DISMANTLING LEVIATHAN

Towards the New Millennium Series

Anthony Westell, *Reinventing Canada,* 1994

David Matas, *No More: The Battle against Human Rights Violations,* 1994

Randall White, *Global Spin: Probing the Globalization Debate,* 1995

Don Waterfall, *Dismantling Leviathan: Cutting Government Down to Size,* 1995

DISMANTLING LEVIATHAN

Cutting Government Down to Size

Don Waterfall

DUNDURN PRESS
Toronto • Oxford

Edited by Tom Kluger
Printed and bound in Canada by Webcom

The publisher wishes to acknowledge the generous assistance and ongoing support of the **Canada Council**, the **Book Publishing Industry Development Program** of the **Department of Canadian Heritage**, the **Ontario Arts Council**, the **Ontario Publishing Centre** of the **Ministry of Citizenship, Culture and Recreation**, and the **Ontario Heritage Foundation**.

Care has been taken to trace the ownership of copyright material used in the text.. The author and publisher welcome any information enabling them to rectify any reference or credit in subsequent editions.

J. Kirk Howard, Publisher

Canadian Cataloguing in Publication Data

Waterfall, Don, 1943–
Dismantling Leviathan : cutting government down to size

(Towards the new millennium series)
Includes bibliographical references and index
ISBN 1-55002-243-1

1. Canada – Politics and government – 1993 – .*
I. Title. II. Series.

JL108.W3 1995 971.064′8 C95-931836-4

Dundurn Press Limited
2181 Queen Street East
Suite 301
Toronto, Canada
M4E 1E5

Dundurn Distribution
73 Lime Walk
Headington, Oxford
England
0X3 7AD

Dundurn Press Limited
1823 Maryland Avenue
P.O. Box 1000
Niagara Falls, N.Y.
U.S.A. 14302-1000

CONTENTS

To Cara and Thomas
and their century

Acknowledgements

I would like to express appreciation to a rather large number of people who, knowingly or not, made this essay possible.

Inevitably, the time taken to plan, research, write and rewrite is time taken away from one's family. The tolerance they have shown to an enterprise that must have seemed bizarre, incomprehensible, and quixotic has been exemplary. On the other hand, they are probably used to my being bizarre, incomprehensible, and quixotic. I also owe all of them my thanks for home computer time – time won in an unfair fight. I am dedicating this essay to my children in the hope that some day they will understand the extent to which it is rooted in my concern about their century.

The second category to which I owe a debt of gratitude is much more amorphous. Included are those who taught me to think about politics and government long ago when I was a student. The extent to which I have kept coming back to classical political philosophy, from Hobbes to Mill and Marx, despite the distractions of an adult life, is a tribute to the passion they instilled in me. It is a curious but undeniable fact that regardless of where they stood in the political spectrum, the most lasting lesson my teachers taught me, by example and by instruction, was respect for freedom of thought.

Included as well are those who started me thinking about the problems of public administration, popular writers on management theory – the dean of them all being Peter Drucker – speakers in numerous courses and seminars I have attended in and around government, and several colleagues too. It is not really possible for me to name them but some of them at least will know who they are. The depth of thought of a number of people in government and, better still, the determination of those few who successfully carry through new ideas are national treasures. I should mention the Canadian Centre for Management Development, which has drawn many facts and ideas to my attention. I think of a morning series known as "Armchair Discussions" which are heavily attended by managers in the Public Service and which I have never known to be trivial or short on thoughtfulness.

I would like to mention Sir Roger Douglas, a former minister of finance of New Zealand, whose vigorous remarks did much to stimulate my thinking, especially on the issue of reform of education.

However, I must reserve my most heartfelt thanks to Robert Rabinovitch, public servant, businessman, thinker, and friend, who read the entire manuscript and provided a great many astute comments and helpful criticisms. Modest as are the attainments of this essay, it is twice as good as it would have been had I not had the benefit of his advice. Besides helping me clarify a number of issues, he launched me into others I would not have thought to address without his prompting. Of course, the observations and conclusions of these pages are my own. He bears no responsibility for my own inept formulations and inferences, still less for those few instances in which I had the temerity to ignore his advice.

It goes without saying that the views expressed in this book are entirely my own and at no time reflect the opinion or policies of any department of government in which I have worked.

INTRODUCTION

I hesitate to begin this essay autobiographically, but its origin and nature are inseparable from personal experience.

For nearly thirty years I have toiled as a public servant. Where I have toiled is of no particular importance and the substance of my career equally unimportant. I have worked in a variety of slots. I am part of the abscess of middle management in the federal bureaucracy and I speak from that point of view, not from the perspective of those who have managed huge departments, been intimate with political leaders or been responsible for great decisions, nor, for that matter, from that of experts in public administration.

I "grew up" in a staunchly bureaucratic environment that I can best typify by using the words that appear on personnel appraisal forms: the plan-organize-control-direct organization. I carried out my tasks and later directed others to carry out theirs. This sort of work tends to make you conservative. You are too busy to cope with change or new ideas because they interfere with work; they keep you from getting on with what you have to do. As a result your purview becomes exceedingly short. You blunder forward in a tunnel. Change comes anyway, forced upon you by circumstance, but it alters you little. Personally, I lost touch with ideas, and I suspect few of my colleagues saw me as an idea man. Ideas always seem impractical unless they are the ones you are occupied with putting into effect.

Nonetheless, since by predilection and education I saw myself as an idea person, I was not at all satisfied with this state of affairs. I compensated as much as I could in my personal life, maintaining my interests in literature, history and thought. Rarely did I spend my leisure hours on subjects that were practical or current.

Then I was placed in a job that had to do with policy and strategic issues. For the first time in my career, I became an outsider to the operational process, a long-range planner and an adviser. I floundered, trying to adapt to a world that was not "in-box" governed. I took the opportunity to learn, all the same, and I began to see practices in government that made no sense. I made halting efforts to improve some of them. I began to take seriously organizational theorists whom, before, I would have treated as low-brow publicists, secular Norman Vincent Peales. Many of my colleagues saw them as impractical theorists floating ridiculous, or at best amusing, ideas. Their good sense, their occasional grasp of history, and their vision of what might lie in the future were striking to me in my increasing thirst for understanding. I attended courses on management and I learned a little – very little, I can say without modesty – about the potential of information technology.

This exceedingly limited stimulation of my consciousness hardly justifies, or qualifies, me to write a book. However, I was becoming more and more engaged. I became appalled at many of the values evident in the bureaucracy, at the waste and purposelessness of many programmes, at the lack of impetus to change unless one was staring down the barrel of a gun – all this despite obvious symptoms of the looming crisis in government, exemplified most prominently by the phenomena of debt and high taxes.

In spirit, I joined those who have come to the conclusion that the role of government has become seriously, even disastrously, skewed. Through decades of mistaken policy, we are now courting catastrophe. Democratic institutions themselves stand in peril. Basic freedoms, in particular the freedom to preserve and enjoy one's own earnings, have been seriously curtailed. The belief of Canadians in their institutions, their sense of public obligation and conformity to law – witness past cigarette smuggling and the black market economy that have come into being to evade the Goods and Services Tax (GST) – are at a low ebb.

I am fully persuaded that "crisis" or even "catastrophe" is the right word to use for this time in our national life, crisis both as calamity and as turning point, an occasion demanding decision and change. We are on the brink of a major upheaval, that much is certain. What is not certain is its direction. There could be a breakdown of authority, national bankruptcy or catastrophic drift – I have heard the word "revolution" uttered by staid middle-class taxpayers. Or there could be renewal, a radical redefinition of politics, a new philosophy of the role of government – the first such overhaul since the advent of the welfare state in this country about sixty years ago. Change in this sense is an opportunity, a chance to right what has gone terribly wrong. Moreover, what is required is so fundamental that it justifies my grandiose title. Perhaps as much as when political philosopher Thomas Hobbes wrote 344 years ago, during revolution and civil war in England, and explosive scientific and philosophical creativity in Western Europe, the state is in desperate need of regeneration.*

We may be pregnant with such a change. Technology, especially information technology, is in the midst of a giant leap forward. Ideas are in the air, even within government. "Downsizing" is an iterative and often discon-

* Hobbes' *Leviathan*, which will be discussed in more detail later on, may be considered the first great work of modern political philosophy (if we except Machiavelli's *The Prince*). Hobbes used Leviathan, the Biblical sea monster, as his symbol of the state, the "sovereign power."

certing reality. Customer service is a buzzword. New concepts of management and of doing business are rife, at least in training circles: "empowerment," non-linear thinking and devolving decision-making, "reengineering." Programme Review has encapsulated, at least in theory, a radical reexamination of the role of the federal government with the object of cutting it down to size. Some departments are implementing major changes. The federal budget of February 1995 provided a blueprint for a phased return to fiscal responsibility.

At least that's the theory. Internal reform of government has a long history of petering out before significant progress is achieved. To read the senior management journals and newsletters, you might think a massive wave is sweeping government, altering practices, saving money, wiping out nests of inefficiency, introducing automated systems, simplifying processes. I wish it were so. A single day in almost any office selected at random will soon free you of the illusion. The management revolution in government is so far a veneer of platitudes, a wispy vapour trail of rhetoric; the reality is one of small-think, self-protection, dissipated morale, obfuscation, and panic-driven workaholism at the top. The obstacles are huge, the bureaucratic vested interests, like the great landowners of post-feudal Europe, are well entrenched and well armed. Transformation of government and politics will require much careful thought and arduous effort. And it will require vision – a much misused word.

It would be too much to expect that the aging machinery of government is up to reforming itself. Radical change tends to come from the outside. It comes often from radical new thinkers who see things in new ways. It also requires a base in broader society, a genuinely public momentum. Democracy offers an opportunity for outsiders to be influential that is unequalled in any other system. It allows mechanisms to bring about change through legitimate means. In a modest way, this happens every time a general election is held. Tired old administrations that have lost their way or become too comfortable in office, like the Liberals of 1957, give way to different, less entrenched political forces. Marcel Massé, a politician who has got the big issues right, has spoken of his jump from the bureaucracy to political life as rooted in a conviction that government needed to be changed in fundamental ways. "I thought that I was more likely to be able to contribute to this process as an elected representative rather than as a deputy minister." He is right, it seems to me, that major change, if it is to come at all, has to be based on strong political leadership.

However, it is still a moot point whether it will come from our politicians. This is for two reasons. The first is that politicians alone can do very little to reform a bureaucracy. The bureaucracy is a huge, barely moveable beast. To get it to move, you must have the enthusiastic support of key senior bureaucrats. No federal government in recent times can have expressed more dissatisfaction with the Public Service than the Mulroney Government, nor has any tried harder to bring reform to bear on it. Yet, its efforts – the Nielsen Report, Public Service 2000 (an initiative designed to promote better client service, among other things, that never made it from the drawing board) – were a dismal failure. By contrast, much more radical change – or, at least, reduction – is now being imposed on the Public Service through Programme Review and budget constraints but, so far, the Chrétien Government has faced only limited opposition and it has some enthusiastic support. Why? The differences seem almost entirely due to the varying levels of trust bureaucrats have or have had in these two parties. Mulroney's forces adopted a stance that was often scathing and adversarial; the Liberals have traditionally projected a more cooperative image.

Secondly, governments are cautious. They live by the latest poll. Ministers have a huge learning curve when they come into office and are heavily dependent on their departments. They have constituencies they have to please and the cumulative effect of the pork-barrel is often to undermine a regime's better intentions. This factor was particularly potent during the Mulroney years and helped prevent the Tories from reaping the benefits from some of their more imaginative schemes. Politicians are faced with big problems every day. No one – certainly I do not – should underestimate what it means to spend sixteen hours a day wrestling with everything under the sun, from the morale of beleaguered blue helmets in Bosnia to the strength of the dollar, and from the needs of welfare mothers to national unity, often with the hot lights of media attention bearing down. Governments do not last very long. Their outlook is rather short term, occasionally a few years or up to the next election, but never more and often less.

As a result, "long-term planning" is a bizarre enterprise in government, an exercise in the fantastic. A former finance minister's comment on the Martin budget – that his government could not have carried out such drastic cuts because the time was not ripe – is a devastating comment on our political system. It suggests that government is incapable of decisive action unless confronted by catastrophe. These are symptoms of our political culture and it would be too idealistic, even irresponsible, to expect politicians to be much different from the way they are.

I do not believe, therefore, that the internal processes of the bureaucracy or the political process will be enough to make the far-reaching change that is required. Whether driven by the force of logic or by my own education and intellectual bent, I reached the conclusion that we need not just changes of government or of government policies, but a change of the basic philosophy of government, a revised concept of what the business of government is, and a change in the political culture in which we all share. Our current crisis is not an accident and not the result of a few mistaken judgments, or the stupidities of one political party or another, or a few years of poor economic performance. It is the outcome of years and years in which a political philosophy that demanded the expansion of government has held sway. It is the product of an idea gone wrong, a system that has run out of steam, in the very real sense that it has overreached the resources and energies it can command to fulfil its tasks. This philosophy needs to be rethought from its very basics.

When we trace the welfare state back to its origins and consider the theory of government that produced it and is responsible for our current problems, we come upon the path not taken, the one we abandoned prematurely. The corrective lies in a better understanding and a more concerted application of this path, principles of liberalism from which the West departed during the last hundred years. I do not mean the "liberalism" of the American left or the "liberalism" of our own party that has adopted that name, but the liberalism that, however much it has been abandoned as the main ideology of government, still lies at the heart of our democratic system, that focuses on individual rights and freedoms and envisages government as an institution appropriate in size and function to the existence and creativity of free individuals. Some people will see mine as a "conservative" point of view. I would reject this label and ask those inclined to apply it to think through their definitions with greater clarity. The highly confused movement in our southern neighbour that calls itself conservative contains liberal and conservative elements. If you can truly find any of the latter in these pages – protection of privilege, preservation of traditional institutions, sacrifice of the poor, a "tough" law-and-order agenda, intolerance of many social and ethnic groups – then I will be very much obliged to you for pointing them out so that I can expunge them from my text.

This essay is a modest and, in a sense, personal contribution toward the analysis of what ails the practice of government in Canada, and toward a vision for change. It is not about moving to the fringes of our political spectrum – it favours no party – but of radically moving its centre. It has little to say about the national issues that our political and journalistic commentators tend to focus on: national unity, free trade, and the like. Those issues are of crucial importance, but even more fundamental issues have descended upon us and demand our attention. This essay is not a comprehensive academic exercise. It is, to say the least, selective in its subject matter and its use of evidence, as seen in its very selective bibliography. I make no special claims of originality. If I were to offer a defence of this approach, it would be to stress the need for coherence, accessibility, and flow of argument. What is important is not merely my arguments but your responses to them, even if you are led to different conclusions from mine. Clarification of thinking and articulate expression of differing points of view can only do us good.

What I will try to do is discuss the dreadful pass of debt and inefficiency that government has reached, and offer some possible directions for reorientation and renewal of government organizations. Diagnosis of the problems of government and some possible remedies, or directions for finding them, will take up the bulk of this essay. The argument will then move on into theory and seek to reestablish the primary importance to our political thought of the liberal tradition. I will seek to demonstrate its essential function in underpinning political and governmental institutions that will serve us and our deepest interests far better than the monstrous creatures that frustrate and often intimidate us now.

CHAPTER ONE

WHERE WILL IT ALL END?

The cost of government is always a political issue but in normal times it is a relative one – relative among other things to the benefits of the programmes or services being offered or the strength, or sometimes the weakness, of the economy. With the huge expansion of the welfare state in the 1960s, things began to change significantly in Canada. The cost of government then started to snowball, and between about 1975 and the present, while we slept, it turned into a monumental concern – *the* monumental concern – no longer merely an issue with pluses or minuses, but the focus of a crisis in our political life.

A few statistics speak more eloquently than reams of prose. The ones I offer are selective and illustrative: they are based mostly on the annual *Canadian Almanacs and Directories* and *Canada Yearbooks.*[1] Statisticians express all sorts of warnings about their numbers, given that over the years many of the concepts and targets of analysis change and because their interpretation depends on a host of factors that cannot be stated or taken into account. I am an amateur, not even a gifted one, but I shall plough on anyway with the boldness of the ignorant. I will draw some comparisons between 1950 and 1990. They leave a lot unsaid, but what they do tell us is still striking.

The two most important indicators of the growth of government in Canada are the increase in number of government employees and the increase in the cost of government as a percentage of GNP or GDP. To these I will come shortly. Although less important, some other facts and statistics may illustrate the growth and diversification of government functions. In 1950, the federal government got along with twenty departments, one more than the number with which it started the year; there were twenty-six in 1990, just before the "streamlining" of the Kim Campbell interregnum. Although not a particularly arresting figure, two others are more impressive. The Cabinet had grown from twenty-one to nearly forty, and the size and responsibilities of the departments were massively greater than their predecessors. The growth in the number of agencies of government mushroomed.[2] About twenty-seven can be counted for 1950 compared with some eighty-five for 1990.

The Campbell and Chrétien Cabinets were much smaller. The Liberals organized the government into twenty-three departments in 1994, and there were also twenty-three ministers. These reductions were in part true economies, not only the modest one of reducing the number of highly paid ministers, but also some bigger organizational ones. Operations that had had more expensive existences as independent entities were forced to share support services. But one should not overestimate the importance of these moves. Huge departments were replaced by still more massive ones. Forced marriages, moreover, engendered a new set of bureaucratic problems that absorbed energies and resources. Disparate areas are forced to find common ground that may exist only in the imagination. Industry Canada, along with its predecessors, is a good example of a department whose successive reorganizations extending back over at least half a decade have been time- and efficiency-consuming. On the other side of the coin, some functional areas, like communications, whose operation within unified agencies made some sense, were split among different departments. A reorganization whose intent was to reduce the amount of interdepartmental bickering and need for coordination may therefore have brought about significantly less real gain than was advertised. The reduction in Cabinet also had its cosmetic side. Besides full Cabinet ministers, there were another eight secretaries of state.

Since I have been an Ontarian for most of my life, let me use Ontario for a provincial perspective. In 1950, the Ontario government of Lesley Frost had sixteen departments headed by fourteen ministers; there were seventeen other agencies of government. By 1990, the number of departments and ministers had almost doubled to twenty-seven. Other agencies apparently increased only to twenty. What appears to have happened is that the departments of government have multiplied and expanded internally, reflecting, one assumes, the gravitational pull of powers toward the provinces. And agencies, literally dozens of boards, commissions, and provincial Crown corporations that had not seen the light of day forty-five years ago, have tended to emerge within them. For example, the Ministry of Transportation is the successor of the old Department of Highways; its responsibilities have gone far beyond highways (which is, in fact, only right); and one of the corporations under it, GO Transit, is itself a large enterprise. In 1994, after ex-premier Bob Rae's Social Contract, there were still twenty-six ministers and twenty ministries, huge conglomerates like their federal counterparts.

Between 1950 and 1990, employment in federal government organizations of all kinds grew by some 340 per cent. If you count only civilians (military growth was limited), the increase has been almost fivefold.[3] These may be measured against an approximate doubling of population. The 1991 census identifies 417,300 employees of government and over 161,000 in government enterprises, for a total of 578,300, which may be compared with the equivalent of about 169,000 in 1950 (including nearly 62,000 in the armed services).[4]

At the end of 1990, 2,692,573 persons worked in all capacities for all levels of government in Canada. About one-fifth of the workforce was employed by some level of government. This is staggering. The federal government is clearly not the biggest culprit: not far off one million worked for each of the provincial and the local levels. Although it is difficult to obtain comparative figures for 1950, and other statistics tend to be contradictory or difficult to interpret, it is obvious that great as the increase at the federal level has been, it has been even greater at the other levels.[5] In fact, the Public Service of Canada proper (that is, leaving out employees of government whose employer is not the Public Service Commission) is reported to have declined by 5 per cent, or 12,000 full-time employees, since 1984 and to be the same size now as it was in 1973. As we now know, it is destined to decline by another 45,000 in the coming three years. This is significant but it will still leave the federal government some 4.5 times larger than in 1950. Because of huge increases in salary and benefits before 1990, the costs of this relatively stable workforce must have grown dramatically, but these too have now plateaued.

We should also take into account that many working in the private sector are directly dependent for their pay on government contracts or grants. The phenomenon known as "contracting out" is increasing the numbers in this category.

Comparing dollar amounts is much more risky. Some figures are unavailable, and in addition, there are difficult inflation and growth factors to take into account. The concept of Gross National Product has been largely supplanted by Gross Domestic Product, normally a somewhat smaller figure since it excludes offshore earnings. The absolute numbers are not nearly as interesting as the proportion of GNP or GDP that they represent. Moreover, we should not lose sight of the fact that governments now perform more services than they did before, and the growth in their cost is in large measure the result of this. We should remember that in 1950 we were paying the private sector for these services, in areas such as medical needs and hopital insurance (if we were using them at all). We may even have been paying more to the private sector than we now pay to governments, as may be the case with medical insurance. For the moment, however, let us focus on the magnitudes because they are by themselves arresting.

The following is based on inflation from 1950 to 1990 of about 680 per cent and real economic growth of some 600 per cent.[6]

Between these years, real growth in federal expenditure was about 950 per cent. If it is a reasonable proposition that when the economy grows government and government services can or should grow along with it, growth in spending has still been about 60 per cent more than growth of the economy. Its proportion of GDP has expanded alarmingly, from some 14.5 per cent to almost twice that, 25 per cent.

Expenditure by all levels of government has been eleven times greater in real dollars and nearly twice as much as growth.[7] Its share of GDP has increased from about 23 per cent to almost half. Even if all the new services provided by government offer full value for the money, or better value than in 1950 when we purchased them from the private sector, this is very troubling indeed. Can it really be that the value of government to us is equal to nearly half the wealth we produce annually?

The cost of health, welfare, and income security has skyrocketed, increasing by almost twenty times. Clearly, it is the chief cause of increased government expenditure at all levels. Medicare arguably provides better value for money than private health insurance – or than funding health services straight out of our pockets – did in 1950. Nevertheless, in all provinces, its costs have been mushrooming beyond the capacity of government budgets to pay for it. The issue of how to make savings is highly controversial, as governments try to adhere to federal guidelines forbidding extra billing and promoting the widest possible coverage.

Other areas of health and welfare have seen constant growth in cost without the mitigating value to the consumer that may be claimed for medicare. Unemployment Insurance payments during the recession of the early 1990s broke the bank. The UIC deficit for 1990–92 was $1.3 billion; it was still $200 million after the downturn had bottomed out in 1992.[8] Much more needs to be said about UIC, but for the moment one observation will be sufficient. At some point during the growth of our welfare state, UIC ceased to be insurance and turned into income support. Small wonder that it has multiplied deficits and increased tax burdens. Federal government reforms of the last year or two have not even begun to address this fundamental confusion.

In 1950, the Canada Yearbook boasted that expenditures by all levels of government on the state welfare system reached an incredible one billion dollars. In 1990/91 total expenditure by governments on health alone was $44.8 billion and on income security programmes $78 billion, for a total of $122.8 billion. Taking into account inflation, these numbers represent a real growth of 1,800 per cent. This is arguably two or three times what we can afford. The share of GDP represented by health costs increased from 5.8 to 9.7 per cent between 1960 and 1990. Governments' share rose from about 2.5 to 6.9 per cent of GDP. Of this amount, the provincial government share increased from 42 to 72 per cent, having peaked at 76 per cent during the 1980s. A traditional charge to government like the cost of hospital administration increased to $20 billion by 1990, almost half of governmental health expenditure.

Granting that not all of these programmes are without value to us, and that some may even have been to our advantage as consumers of services, have we taxpayers received adequate value for money for this massive growth in programmes and their funding as a whole? Has there been growth in productivity to match dollar growth, as there has been in the private sector?

We have had to pay for this massive growth somehow. We have done it in two ways, through tax hikes and borrowing.

Tax creep in Canada has not been continuous, but the general trend has been for more and more of our economic resources to be taxed. In 1950, a fiscally conservative federal government still trying to reduce the tax burden of the war years collected about $1.3 billion in income taxes. This was 7 per cent of GNP and 7.5 per cent of GDP. The proportion has increased dramatically, probably doubled. Meanwhile, the concept of provincial income tax was in its infancy in 1950; the amounts were small and the tax systems are barely comparable. In 1993, Rae's last tax hike, Ontario's tax bite had reached a crushing 58 per cent of federal tax. In 1950 there were no provincial sales taxes in Canada and, of course, no GST, although hidden sales taxes on some products were relatively steep.

What is disturbing is the small remnant of disposable income left in the pockets of the average wage earner after taxes and other more or less mandatory hits. Of course, we are about six times as wealthy now as we were in 1950, so we have more money to spend after taxes than our fathers and mothers had. But I say "disturbing" because our overall increase in wealth has not been matched by an increase in our freedom to expend that wealth.

Let us take a person of above-average income of, say about $77,000, with a non-working spouse and two children. After claiming normal exemptions and tax credits, let us assume a net income of $59,180, so that none of this would have been taxed by the federal authorities at higher than 26 per cent in 1994. This person, according to the charts, pays $12,722 in federal tax. To this would be added $382 (rounded) in surtax. In Ontario, this person paid $7,379 in provincial income tax and $319 in surtax.

The total income tax, therefore, is

$12,722
$382
$7,379
$319
$20,802

After income tax, the wage earner has over $56,000 left.

We are far from finished. Other huge deductions are made at source. Leaving aside deferred income, such as pensions, our wage earner paid up to $1,162 for Unemployment Insurance, which is a tax, plain and simple. Of course our taxpayer received a tax credit for this amount. So deductions from pay are $21,964. Takehome pay has sunk to about $55,000.

The taxpayer must have owned a house or rented, and therefore, directly or indirectly, paid property taxes to the municipal authorities. Even if this person was not hit by "market valuation," some $3,000 will have been loaded onto the tax bill. This is a modest estimate for a person of $77,000 income. And this money the homeowner pays in local tax has already been subject to federal and provincial income tax – there is no exemption for taxes paid to municipal authorities. This is grossly unfair. The only excuse for it is that it means more tax money for these levels of government. The reason is rapacity. There is tax upon a tax (as the GST on postage stamps is, but for the sleight of hand of turning Canada Post into a Crown corporation). But this is an aside.

At this point the wage earner still has a hefty $52,000 or so in pocket. I am afraid not. With that money, the person makes purchases other than food totalling perhaps $15,000 per year. Of this, 15 per cent of the original value of the goods and services was paid in federal and provincial sales tax if the person lived in Ontario. So our luckless taxpayer has shelled out nearly another $2,000 to governments. For the years 1993 and later, many insurance premiums were made subject to Ontario provincial sales tax, adding some $300 to the annual bill. We have now reached some $27,300 in deductions, all of it paid to governments, and have left our wage earner with less than two-thirds of his or her gross income.

The person has less than $50,000 left. Miscellaneous payments to governments – licenses, postage stamps, public utilities, public transportation (counting GST on some of these) – are hard to estimate. Let us use the relatively arbitrary figure of $5,000 for our wage earner. These should be counted in because they are payments to governments for their services. Disposable income is now about $45,000, and some 42 per cent of gross income has been paid to governments in one way or another for their products and services. Any other earnings the taxpayer makes – from term investments, second jobs, and the like – will be taxed at the highest rate (less, under current rules, for capital gains and dividend income). In Ontario, this is now an incredible 52 to 53 per cent. Does it provide the wage earner with the incentive to work harder or invest his or her income to make more money?

I do not have ready comparisons with 1950 for all of these tax-bites but, at any rate, it is easy to see how governments' share of the value of what we produce doubled over these forty years.

Now, this is a well-off family. Lower down the income ladder, wage earners will pay less tax as a percentage of gross income but also have less disposable income after tax is paid. Higher up the economic ladder, at the 29 per cent rate and with additional tax surcharges, a portion of income will be taxed at a still higher rate. Deputy Minister of Finance David Dodge recently said that taxation by all levels of government in Canada has reached 40 per cent, giving us the dubious honour of being the second most heavily taxed people in the Group of Seven, behind France.[9] This is about twice the figure for 1950, looking at gross figures for tax revenue divided by GNP. In other words, whichever way we look at it, we come out with about the same picture of the cost of government.

As the tax-load and the deficit have mushroomed, a corresponding, exceedingly illiberal ideology has grown up in government. Governments have come to believe that their taxing power is virtually unlimited, that personal income is a public asset and what is left in individual hands is a sort of allowance, pocket money bestowed by a generous parent. Their response to the limitless needs of the budget has almost always been to raise taxes or find other ways of expanding revenue. Perhaps the 1995 budget should be seen as an exception, in view of its significant reductions in departmental budgets. But in general, governments view taxpayers as adversaries and treat them with a brusqueness and high-handedness that smacks of the arbitrary. Now, in saying this I do not doubt that there are many wrongdoers among taxpayers. There are many people who misreport income deliberately or use every possible trick, illegal or of questionable legality, to avoid paying tax. This is a particular problem in the private sector and a bigger problem still in its upper reaches. The tone of relations between the sovereign power and the members of society is, as I shall often have occasion to point out in the pages to come, set by the worst among us, and adequate means of enforcement are crucial if government finances are to be on a sound basis. But do these factors justify treating everyone, especially the vulnerable, as if they are convicted criminals? Let me give a few examples.

The previous government amended the Income Tax Act to require certain people not in receipt of normal employment earnings – contract personnel or people with fairly large investment income – to pay taxes by instalments, four times per year. This is reasonable in many instances; dishonest people should not be able to slip out of their duty to pay taxes in a timely fashion. However, the government requires such instalments even if the taxpayer has received no income during the taxation year up to the time of the first instalment and regardless of whether he or she can estimate his or her total income at the beginning of the year, something difficult for people with irregular incomes to do. What must the taxpayer do, borrow in order to pay tax on non-existent income? If you point out these anomalies to the authorities, you get back a "threatening letter," saying the law is the law and failure to comply with it can result in interest levies or other penalties.

A story in a local Ottawa magazine is equally disturbing.[10] A street vendor who had come off social assistance and made a success of a hot-dog business erred rather substantially in reporting some of his income. When he was queried by the taxation authorities, he stated he had been ignorant of the tax rules and was willing to pay his arrears promptly. However, his case having been put into the hands of the special investigations unit, not merely tax auditors, he was levied not only his arrears and heavy interest, but an additional punitive penalty totalling some $40,000, on the presumption that he acted deliberately. According to the article, a local MP expressed sympathy but said that you could not allow people to escape tax obligations simply by claiming ignorance. But this is not the point. What is disturbing is the lack of due process and the lack of protection of rights afforded to small operators. The taxation authorities are able to exact penalties without having to prove intent on the part of a putative violator of the tax laws. In this instance, the article goes on to say, even the judicial authorities upheld this principle. Our very judicial system, the arbiter and protector of our rights, waives them with impunity when the issue is taxation.

Of concern in both these examples is that the people they most often hurt are little people with small amounts of income. Street vendors are said to make, on average, about $35,000 a year. Contractors are often spouses or small entrepreneurs struggling to find work and never knowing where the next contract may come from. By contrast, to my knowledge there are very rich people who pay little or nothing in taxes. If the long promised "minimum tax" has been put into effect, the event has escaped my notice. Our governments have been singularly duplicitous on the issue of fairness in the tax system: they beat up on low-income earners and put the squeeze on the middle class, but consistently cave in to the financial might of the wealthy.

The grasping nature of government has extended even to elected officials, our democratic representatives, even "conservative" ones, not just their advisers in the civil services. A Parliamentary committee's mid-1994 recommendations on "replacement" of the GST was an example of this. The committee suggested a cosmetic reduction in the rate, to be made up by extending the tax to all purchases, even food. It was not government officials or even Cabinet ministers who came up with this insulting "reform," which would hit everyone harder (especially the poor) since it would tax daily necessities, but our ordinary elected representatives. It is small wonder that they have led us into not only an economic crisis but a political one, a crisis of legitimacy.

Having run out of resources to tax, governments have turned to the money-lenders to make up their shortfalls. The indebtedness of governments, the astronomical deficits that are piled up year by year, and a gross national debt that in Canada is approaching a year's Gross Domestic Product are well known to practically everyone.[11] They are daily fare in the media. Almost one-quarter of federal government expenditure went to pay interest on the national debt in 1992/93, accounting for more than the annual budgetary deficit. We are borrowing money to pay principal and interest on money we have borrowed. Moreover, a fair, though not massive, portion of this debt is owed to foreigners.

In 1950, the national debt inherited from the war was high. The gross national debt was $16.8 billion – net* was $11.6 billion – out of a Gross National Product of $18.1 billion, or 92.5 per cent, and a GDP of $16.9 billion, or 100 per cent to all intents and purposes.[12] Net national debt per capita was calculated to be about $850. But the St. Laurent government acted with exemplary prudence. The one-time bonanza from demobilization had already been exploited in the immediate post-war years; now it was a clear matter of proper management of finite resources. The government's expenditures of about $2.5 billion in 1950 included debt servicing of some $450 million and after that there was actually a surplus of some $130 million. Surpluses are also recorded for 1951 and 1952. A government that had gone deeply into debt to wage war was behaving responsibly in peacetime by decreasing the debt load through balanced budgets.

Through growth, careful management of the fisc, and continued rapid demobilization, the 1950 numbers came down, in relative terms, during the subsequent decade, so that gross national debt was $20.1 billion and net $12.1 billion, against a GNP of $35.9 billion, $676 per capita, in 1960 during the Diefenbaker years. At constant prices, the gross national debt had actually declined to $14.8 billion, net to $8.9 billion. Gross national debt was less than 60 per cent of GNP.

In 1990/91 gross federal debt was $443.3 billion and net $385 billion. If the net liabilities of the other two levels of government are added, the national debt was about $550 billion gross and $483 billion net. Gross national debt was, in other words, about five-sixths of GDP. In the last half of 1994, a figure of $680 billion is being used, very nearly equal to GDP. The only good thing to be said about the 1990 figure is that it is a lower proportion than in 1950, though net debt appears to have exceeded that of

*Net debt = gross debt minus the government's assets (property, buildings, equipment, etc.).

1950. If we were capable of the same financial prudence now as then, we might yet be able to turn things around. But the trend lines are running in opposite directions. In 1950 government was in surplus and had to foot the bill for only a fraction of the bureaucracy and programmes our governments pay for now. In 1990, on the brink of recession, public indebtedness was already out of control, though we took years to recognize the fact. Our problem would be more difficult than theirs of 1950 even if we had their good sense.

How did this catastrophe occur?

It is the result of more than a generation of cumulative mismanagement. John Maynard Keynes advised that in tough times it was acceptable for governments to go mildly into debt in order to help the economy out of recession. In good times, the policy was to be reversed: the debt was to be paid off and expenditure pulled back. However, governments have broken nearly all the rules. They believed growth and progress were inevitable, but nothing is inevitable. They also believed that a greater involvement of government in the economy, even in management and ownership of enterprises, was a good thing, not the wasteful luxury we now know most of it to have been. They moved into many areas and stayed in others at the very time they were trying to finance an expensive new social security system. They got into the habit of deficit spending in good times as well as bad, and came to believe that this was the key to avoiding hard times altogether. Small deficits were slightly inflationary but induced growth, which more than paid off the debts incurred earlier. Or so the theory said.

The policy did not work badly in the boom years of the 1950s and 1960s. It came a cropper in the hyperinflationary 1970s, the years of "stagflation," when slow economic growth went side by side with astronomical price inflation and higher unemployment and welfare outlays, and during the major recessions of the early 1980s and 1990s. Costly government programmes, some of them highly questionable (what did governments have to do with funding private advocacy groups?), overspending in prosperity and finding the coffers empty when hard times set in, caused the increasing cycles of indebtedness that have now reached truly critical proportions. Not learning their lesson, governments have gone on to tax at precisely the times when it was most crucial to leave money in people's pockets, as Rae's NDP government did in Ontario in 1993.

Not only at federal level but in the provinces, deficits have proliferated. Provinces have often sought, but failed to achieve, balanced budgets because of the limitations on their tax base, and they were therefore traditionally cautious spenders. This is reflected in their relatively modest portion of the national debt. Nevertheless, this caution was thrown to the winds in the

1980s. The cumulative provincial deficits for 1994 were projected in media reports at $17 billion. In 1990 the provincial share of the national debt was about $75 billion, mushrooming to $127 billion in 1993. In 1995, one province after another announced balanced budgets but the exceptions, Ontario and Quebec, represent the lion's share of Canada's population and economy.

The impact on our economy of both indebtedness and the size and cost of government have been disastrous. First, a sizeable per centage of taxes and of the GDP is wasted on unproductive debt repayment and interest payments, much of these to foreign lenders. Secondly, our competitiveness is undermined. In Japan, where the national debt is said to be about 3 per cent of GDP, a tiny fraction of Canada's, nearly all the funds we waste can be left in taxpayers' pockets or spent on public works during recession (the Japanese have been true and effective Keynesians), putting a few people to work and investing in infrastructure for the future when it will be needed. Thirdly, the dominance of our economy by the public sector introduces large-scale inefficiencies. The inefficiency of government departments and public enterprises has long been a right-wing cliché, but, alas, one borne out by the available evidence. The service sector generally is weak in productivity, and government dominates that sector. Finally, not only is the freedom of individual Canadians to dispose of their resources subject to a tight clamp, the range of effective choice reduced, but the ability of consumers to spend our way toward some relief has been seriously decreased by unemployment and high tax levels.

No business or family could survive with the debt load we bear as a result of government spending. Imagine if you spent 98 per cent of your pay one year, and in each of the next ten you received a pay raise of 4 per cent a year but your spending increased by 5 or 6 per cent a year! At the end of the ten years you would be spending close to ten per cent more than you earn, and you would have a fat debt service bill equal to a much higher percentage of your income. A private company following a similar policy would, broadly speaking, be in the same position, and would be bankrupt after several years of heavy borrowing without a concomitant increase in profits. But governments and their servants are by and large blind to this perspective, hiding behind clichés about the differences between the public and the private sector, the collective and the individual, and boasting, "Well, we are still here, aren't we?" They are still here, like the aristocracy on the eve of the French Revolution.

The concept of bankruptcy does not apply readily to the public sector. Governments can go on borrowing and getting more and more deeply into debt, and still survive for a very long time. The collapse of governments that run out of the resources to meet their commitments is rare. This should not give any of us a sense of relief. It does not mean that our current situation is not catastrophic. It means that, as in many other ways, the means of measuring catastrophe in the public sector are elusive. Government can continue to operate under a shroud of "business as usual," as the Tories did while the deficit mounted through the 1980s and early 1990s.

If the national debt is owed largely to domestic institutions, the seriousness of the situation may be masked even more. Italy has larger public debt than Canada, for example, but its creditors are virtually all domestic institutions, which share their government's desire for mutual survival and are more responsive to the national will. If a sizeable proportion of the debt is foreign, the situation changes. Once international lending institutions decide that they can no longer tolerate a debtor country's fiscal mismanagement, they tend to intervene in its domestic affairs and dictate fiscal and economic policy until the situation is rectified. This happened to New Zealand in the 1980s – Australia, too, seems to have acted to reduce its indebtedness to foreigners, in order to avoid external interference – and it is this that comes closest to public sector bankruptcy. Are we so far away? We can avoid such subjugation by showing we can get our own house in order, but already both federal and provincial governments have lost triple-A status as borrowers in the eyes of foreign lenders. As a consequence, the interest rates we have to pay for borrowed money have gone up.

There have been many numbers in the preceding pages and my intention that the presentation be graphic and simple may not have been achieved. Let me sum up a few of the main points.

Taking cost as a good measure of size, government at all levels in Canada has grown at a rate approximately twice as fast as the economy and has doubled its share of GDP. Much of this has been due to the vast increase in state welfare systems, which have grown faster than the rest of government operations. Traditional elements, like the hospital system, have grown much more costly – I estimated the increase for this sector overall at over threefold. At the same time, governments got into all sorts of other areas, little recognizing how expensive the commitment to social welfare was to be. The revenue required to fuel this growth has led governments, according to some sources, to siphon 40 per cent of annual income from Canadians, a staggering representation of the extent of government domination of our lives. Even so, massive borrowing has been necessary to top up public coffers, so that the national debt is now estimated to be nearly equal to GDP. It would take a whole year's worth of all that Canadians earn to pay it off.

Governments are, or act as if they are, immune to normal measures of success and failure. What are some of the measures of catastrophe? Public indebtedness, to take perhaps our principal problem, magnifies the cost of government and the economic harm done by government. By forcing up taxation rates, governments restrict private expenditure – and the role it can have in stimulating the economy – and limit our competitiveness in the international market place. Moreover, government has so overreached and overspent itself that it can no longer play a positive role during hard times. It has run out of resources that could be used for economic stimulus during recession. The Chrétien Government's infrastructure programme would be sensible in any normal circumstances. Politically, both during and since the 1993 election campaign, the promise of jobs has been astute and a confidence-builder; the programme has been administered with some discretion and sensitivity. But economically this was the wrong time. The billions this programme has added to the national debt far outweigh the modest political, economic and social benefits it may bring.[13]

But why have we allowed government to grow to such a size that it has landed us in this pit? Why is government so costly? Part of the answer to this is that government has taken too much on. Another part of the answer is that government is inefficient and wasteful. It is costly to run and poor at showing value for money.

Why? Among the elements of governmental bureaucracy that add to its overhead are excessive hierarchy, inflexible management, a layered and convoluted system of financial accountability that costs rather than saves money, duplication of functions and services, and the splitting of work among large numbers of units within and among departments. In parallel with these organizational blockages goes a bureacratic psychology: overcaution, indecision, buck-passing, obsequiousness, turf mentality, "empire-building," cover-up. No definitive or persuasive measurement exists to tell us whether governments are healthy and effective, as profits show the health of private businesses.

Let us now look at these assertions in more detail.

CHAPTER TWO

Exposing Leviathan

The great failure of government over the years has been its inability to provide efficient services to the public or to act decisively and visibly in the public interest. These statements may appear paradoxical. The *raison d'être* of the public sector is to serve the public interest. Socialists and progressives have long held that it is the private sector that is self-serving and that we can only trust enterprises that are publicly owned or operated to serve the public interest judiciously and fairly as a matter of course. This view stood behind calls for nationalization in earlier days. However, it is one thing to say an entity is bound to serve the public interest and quite another for it to do so in practice.

Private companies indubitably exist for their own profit. There have been many instances of their making their money and running, paying little attention to long-term customer satisfaction or well-being. "You bought it and it's no longer my responsibility" is a familiar enough refrain that has been heard everywhere from car showrooms to the corner store. Enough of these stories continue to be heard to make any shopper wary. Nevertheless, the private sector usually serves its customers, in the sense of meeting their wishes, better than public sector organizations serve the broad public. The private sector is subject to the iron law of the market place: if a company fails to satisfy its customers better than others can satisfy them, they can go elsewhere and it will soon be out of business. The very longstanding practice of a company like Eaton's to take back merchandise with few questions asked and no hassle is one of the secrets of its century of success.

In recent years, the North American private sector has had to retool itself extensively in the face of foreign competition and much more demanding consumers. The changes are often revolutionary, creating models of client service and of the fully customer-oriented organization that go far beyond anything previously known. But the public sector lags. There has in general been little incentive for monopolistic organizations to improve customer service. A recent controversy over cable TV is just the latest of a long series of examples. Having a monopoly, such companies come only after a storm of criticism to the realization that they have offended their public. And then they act to preserve their monopoly rather than simply to provide good service to customers who might take their business elsewhere. In government, programmes designed to improve service to the public and other streamlining efforts – Public Service 2000, for example – have often been halting and perfunctory. Mere lip-service has been paid to them.

To be fair, some departments are trying. Particularly in the last few years, the pressure of the deficit and comparisons with the private sector have brought about heightened consciousness of the need for change. Management courses and newssheets are full of buzzwords about client service and "one-stop shopping." Some major projects are under way, in particular the redesign of income security programmes by the Human Resources Department. But these changes are, so far, skin deep. Customer orientation reforms in income security have a very long way to go. Full implementation of an automated system is years away and quite untested. Currently, programmes like the Old Age Pension are mired in a nightmarish hole of backlogs, inefficiency, and unresponsiveness. Meanwhile, the vast majority of officials are not touched by these reforms at all. Far from being irreversible, progress toward client orientation is watered down and patchy.

Why? It is principally because the bureaucracy is set in an ancient mould that is, on the whole, indifferent to quality of service. The same dominant organizational type has served for all kinds of government processes, whether policy-oriented or service-oriented. What are the characteristics of this organizational type and why does it perform so badly?

Public sector organizations, in particular the departments of government, are organized in boxes – boxes within boxes within boxes. "Box" organizations divide work into a sequence of smaller parts and distribute it among units – smaller boxes.

A box is managed by a boss who sets the tasks, monitors work, and is responsible to someone higher up, a superior or the manager of a more inclusive box, for the completion of his or her unit's tasks. Box managers are far from all-powerful, but within their units they plan and organize the work and are responsible for getting it done. They may also have to work with other box managers to fit their parts of the puzzle into the total design of the project. But their superiors, more senior managers, have primary responsibility for planning and coordinating the work of a chain of boxes.

Box structures have characteristics that I will address later. Two points I would like to make here.

First, despite all the talk about goals and objectives that has come with the planning jargon of the "management by objectives" era, boxes tend to be driven by a specific task, rather than goals. They are given a task, frequently misnamed their "objective," and they have to do it. It is their job. You do, as the saying goes, what you have to do. They are therefore said to be task-driven. In a fully goal-driven model, a broad objective would be set and ingenuity would be required to establish means to achieve it. A unit's success would be judged in accordance with its results, the achievement of its target. But ingenuity can get you into trouble. There is risk. It is frequently easier to do what you are told, even if you fail. If you fail, you can always produce a million reasons why, even blaming the manager for setting an unrealistic task. If you fail to achieve a goal, you open yourself to the charge that you are stupid or incompetent or uncreative. No one wants to be told that.

Secondly, there is the inherent inefficiency of dividing work up and putting it back together again. No one at the working level has an overview of the whole process. The left hand does not know what the right hand is doing. Only a superior sees the activity as a whole, but as the job becomes more complex it becomes harder and harder for the more senior managers to have an effective handle. Other units holding a part of the puzzle may not give it the same priority as their cousins or may be less efficient, so that the completion of a whole project will depend on the efficiency of the weakest component. Or, if the project involves successive stages and hand-offs as in an assembly line, the total time needed to complete it will consist of the sum of the time spent on it by all the units plus the time used – effectively lost – in the hand-offs. These losses are usually horrendous, amounting to the majority of the time spent on the process in many cases. Making such a process work demands horizontal activity by the unit manager or his staff, who must liaise with their counterparts to facilitate workflow or to coordinate production. But this means crossing into someone else's jurisdiction. Thus, it often involves intervention by the next level up, at any rate when problems occur that cannot be resolved at the box level. These problems may stem from many sources: lack of knowledge in one box of what is done in another, organizational jealousies ("This is my box, I am responsible for it. Why have you got your sandpail in it?"), different levels of competence, and so on.

A typical example is business travel. The process has been simplified in many agencies, so practice may vary and be less cumbersome than in the past. Nevertheless, travel may involve many different functions, most of them performed by different units in serial order: policy approval (the manager or sometimes two levels of management, and sometimes also a second specialized unit), preparation of a form requesting authority to travel and money for tickets and other travel expenses (the manager, the traveller, a secretary), checking the form, and verifying the availability of funds (budget unit), making travel arrangements (the traveller, a secretary or a travel unit, and a travel agent), issuing tickets (travel agent), issuing an advance (cheque-producers and distributors). After the trip is completed: preparing a form to account for travel expenditures (traveller, secretary), checking and approval (the manager), checking and recording expenditures (budget unit), processing reimbursement of an advance, or amounts owed to the traveller (accounts payable), cutting a cheque, if necessary, a financial audit. I count some thirteen steps involving six to eight different functional units and at least three references upward for management approval – more if managers of other units need to be involved. If someone on the pipeline has a full in-basket, or is slow, ill, or incompetent, the process comes to a standstill. If checking uncovers a problem, there may be a reference backward along the chain. A game of ping-pong may develop. The accounting process can take months and auditors still come back with questions or demands months after that.

If the process involves service to the public, the service is likely to be slow and inadequate. Who is there who knows enough about the whole process to give a complete response to an enquiry on the first go? More likely, the person receiving the call will say, "I don't know that and I will have to get back to you," or, worse still, "That's not my department. Try Madame X." And then, helpfully, "Here is her number." To prove it to yourself, try starting with a city telephone directory – nothing more – and seek information from a municipal government about a building permit involving a minor variance. Or go to city hall and make the rounds yourself. Don't forget your sneakers. At the end of the first week, you will understand why the handiest of home-renovators hire expensive contractors and architects to do their rounds for them.

Now, the process may work well in some cases and less well – bureaucrats would be loath to say badly – in others. However, it is inherently inefficient. This is because it involves so much wasted energy. Every instance of lateral box-hopping takes energy and time. Every movement upward to a third party, the superior, and back down again takes even more energy and time. Because so many players are involved, the potential for delay, for duplication and for error requiring work to be redone is enormous. This is most easily seen again, in the example of validating a travel claim, which hops to a minimum of four or five players (who are sometimes geographically separated), sits in in-baskets for inordinate periods of time and can involve ceaseless wrangling over pennies.

Task-orientation is also a morale-deflator. Those who see only a piece of the action and do not have a clear idea of why they are doing what they do, what their work is for in the larger context, are unlikely to be highly motivated or keen about their work. They will not feel that they are trusted to know the higher purpose of their jobs. This situation is rampant in the military, where an order is justification enough for doing something. Satisfaction must come from getting a task done. Sisyphus, by the same token, should be delighted every time he succeeds in rolling his immense rock to the top of the hill, even though it rolls down and he has to do it all over again. The worker may be stimulated by punishments and other sanctions, but sanctions are invariably a poor motivational tool. They should be kept for unethical conduct or for poor performance out of the ordinary. No one produces well under threat or as a result of fear.

Box structures are hierarchical. They form pyramids. Boxes fit into larger boxes and have boxes within or under them. There is a hierarchy of managers, each responsible to one higher until you reach senior management or the deputy minister, who may be seen, depending on your point of view, as outside all boxes or as the manager of the biggest, most inclusive box.

In a representative department, there could be five or six layers from the top to the bottom: department, branch, bureau, division, section, staff. In another model I am familiar with: agency, area, group, section, unit, desk, staff. Larger bureaucracies, as in Washington, have even more layers, a dozen or more. De-layering, which was a fad of the Public Service 2000 era, was and is largely ineffective. It may have removed some layers here or there, but it had little impact on the Public Service as a whole. Some de-layering was purely cosmetic. In one department, it was declared that the objective of reduction to four managerial layers had been reached because deputy directors in divisions did not count.

The failure of de-layering was partly because the effort tackled a symptom rather than the root causes endemic to box structures. Large organizations of the traditional kind require a certain ratio of managers to staff to assign, check, and coordinate work, or, at least, few have seen an option to this. Personnel policies or the expectations created by them also got in the way. Officials seeking promotion demand experience in "supervision" to help them achieve the next level. Moreover, middle managers give no support to ventures that might rob them of position, status or their jobs.

What I would like to focus on for the present is the inherent inefficiency of hierarchy. The weight of the ladder of authority is oppressive. Managers up the line are expected to "add value" to the products of their subordinates; they therefore frequently feel bound to change them or deliver a string of instructions, directives or creative suggestions. Managers on different rungs of the same ladder frequently duplicate, and just as frequently contradict, one another's work. Everyone in a governmental bureaucracy has had the experience of receiving different or contradictory direction from managers up the line, or of managers going around their immediate subordinates to meddle in work lower down.

On the other hand, even when the system works as it is supposed to in theory, the time lost as recommendations mount from one level to the next is enormous. Managers at lower levels have little incentive to take responsibility in their own hands. It is easier to pass the buck upward and more risky to do something which a superior may disagree with and nail the subordinate for. In theory, the "value added" at each level perfects the product more and more, for example, a memorandum going to a minister. However, in practice, words changed at one level get changed back at another. The amount of time taken to process the item affects its relevance and timeliness so that the perfect product may require radical revision anyway once it has reached the top. A law of organizations is, the more hands, the more error. Certainly there is more opportunity for error and by the laws of probability there will therefore be more error. The phenomenon known as the ombudsman is not a sign that our times are more fastidious than others, but that our times produce more mess than others because of the labyrinthine processes of big government.

"Perfection" may be achieved at the cost of sharpness of focus; cautious senior managers may eliminate the controversial and go with the bland. Surely fewer hands could produce as good results: why should six levels add more value than three? And, if some product is a bit rough, wouldn't the overall efficiency and effectiveness of the organization be improved if more work got finished faster? Surely the frequency of good results would increase and significantly outweigh the bad. But this view is unacceptable to most managers, who are desperately frightened of the consequences of error. You have to get policy right, we are told. That is true enough but what is usually meant by "right" is risk-free, foolproof – unattainable qualities.

Finally, the distance between the top of the organization and the staff at the bottom – who do the real work and possess most of the knowledge – is vast and practically unbridgeable. People at the bottom are subject to so many layers of supervision that they work with a huge and heavy burden of oversight and little contact with senior levels. Junior officials today are said to be the best educated and most able generation government has ever seen. The top dogs are usually smart, but no one, however smart, can know everything going on in an organization. In the best organizations, channels exist to make sure that senior managers know what they need to know. More often, when the crisis occurs and the senior manager finds himself without information that he needs, a scramble takes place. Middle managers may react by pumping more information upstairs for a time to cover their behinds, but this is counterproductive because it further clogs the system and provides more than any senior manager, however brilliant, can be expected to absorb or remember when he needs it.

Hierarchy is a class structure. People are judged by where they sit. Their skills and capacities and performance are evaluated in accordance with their level. "So-and-so is only a '2'" tells you all you need to know about him or her in many bureaucracies. It dictates behaviour. I hesitate to count the number of times I have seen people demeaned by their superiors, whether or not in front of others, simply because they are "junior," and therefore less worthy. People who are the victims of this system come to accept these judgments as their own. And a cycle of self-doubt, depression, and ineffectiveness begins.

A word needs to be said about the heads of the departments themselves, the ministers, elected officials, and their impact on the organizations that serve them. Hierarchical organizations are pyramids pointing upward; ministers are their pinnacles. The task of a department is to glorify its minister and please him or her, well, not forever but as if the minister were to last forever. Departments jump when ministers command, though ministers are rarely satisfied with their officials. Besides the organizational causes for this, real deficiencies in the bureaucratic process, this state of affairs has to do with the different outlooks that politicians and bureaucrats have.

Ministers are, for the time they are in office, people of immense power. They are like kings; they rule territories bigger, more populous and much wealthier than any medieval kingdom. They barely have private lives. They are driven off their feet by the demands of their public lives, which involve constituency and party matters over and above their governmental duties. Their power and their sphere of action are personal and their patterns of thought intuitive, not abstract and "linear" as they are in bureaucracies. Many come to government with no experience of directing organizations as huge as those they are appointed to govern. If they are tempted at all by the trappings of power – and it is a common human weakness – they will develop airs and become still more exalted and more demanding. Enormous energies are expended by the bureaucracy to keep them informed, plan their activities and respond to their needs. The senior levels of departments are particularly taken up with ministers' time. They are always at ministers' elbows, providing them with facts and ideas and keeping them out of trouble. If a minister gets into trouble, he bears the responsibility – but privately may blame the officials.

Anyone would be guilty of abysmal judgment who questioned the essential rightness of this social order. Departments are oriented upward to do the bidding of those on high. That is their natural function. Practically all officials view this as an inseparable aspect of public service; the alternative is unimaginable.

This is a very important fact of life for bureaucracies, one whose meaning we shall have to examine in detail later, and it has important implications for those who talk about customer service in government. The essential confusion is embodied in a line, often heard, that "the Minister is our most important customer." It is certainly true that the minister is the person whom officials primarily serve but this ditty only shows that those who use it do not understand what customer service is. Indeed, this extraordinary confusion does more than anything else to explain why Public Service 2000 failed. "minister" means "servant," etymologically, and in theory the minister is the public's principal servant (actually, when the word was first used for government officials, the service was probably intended for the king). But in practice they are masters. Their ability to command and draw upwards the resources and obedience of their organizations are potent reasons why government bodies are not effectively oriented to serve customers.

Box organizations are territorial. Every unit develops its own interests and seeks advantage for itself. The unit's primary imperative is to defend its turf, maintain its existence, and even expand when it can find opportunities to do so. Every unit engages in a contest, a war, at least to the extent of having to defend itself against the predators and expansionists elsewhere in the system. It is not that everyone is rapacious, but it only takes a few to infect the whole system. This may be put in a "law" with both a strong and a weak form. The law of the maximization of turf states that: Bureaucratic units tend to expand their turf. The weak form is: Units tend to resist encroachments by others and defend their existing turf. This is the law of the integrity of turf.

A related law is: Discrete organizational units tend to serve, in the first instance, their own interests. Hereafter this will be called the law of serving number one. A corollary is that such organizations tend not to serve their customers' or clients' interests as their first priority. Turf is one of the attributes of government that lie at the root of its failure to be an effective service organization.

This law mirrors in some respects the law first enunciated in *Leviathan* by Thomas Hobbes concerning the "natural condition of mankind," Hobbes' version of the state of nature (though Hobbes' law was about individuals). Hobbes concluded that the state of nature was a state of war of everyone against everyone, because everyone has equality of desire and no one has security of his own possessions. For at least defensive reasons, people must fight to subdue others or they may not survive. "Because some ... pursue [conquests] farther than their security requires, if others that otherwise would be glad to be at ease within modest bounds should not by invasion increase their power, they would not be able, long time, by standing only on their defense, to subsist."[1] In other words, it is not because all players, individually or collectively, are aggressive and greedy that there is a war of "all against all"; simple defensiveness against the handful who are aggressive produces the same result.

There is no exaggeration or overdramatization in this image. No one working in the bowels of an organization, short of un-Hobbesian dishonesty or self-deception, would fail to recognize this as the world within which he or she works. People routinely refer to big, branch-size bodies as "baronies." "Bailiwick" is a frequently used expression. The first word you hear from your first boss is of the need to watch out for expansionists and ensure that your own unit's legitimate mandate is defended or enhanced. It is implied, if not explicitly stated, that you will be judged by your ability to carry out these orders. Of course, the smaller the unit, the smaller is the range of opportunity to act as a discrete entity, since such units are responsible to a higher unit that must meld the interests of all its sub-units into a whole. But such tendencies greatly increase the difficulty of coordination by the higher level.

Turf wars are probably the most significant waste of time and energy in government. One ambitious bully can cause a huge cast of characters to enter the fray to fight him off, or die trying. Such conflict is almost always hopelessly unproductive. However rational a change in organizational structure or responsibilities, turf is never given up without a fight. Intervention from above, given that a senior manager occupies broader turf and will be predisposed to seek its best interests as a whole, can resolve such matters, but only with patient strategy and yet more time. And, of course, the senior manager too has her rivals, her need to defend her own much larger turf and her ambition to expand it.

In fact, caution usually rules. Conquest is resisted stoutly because everyone is threatened by it. The effects of stamping out aggressors, however, are themselves negative. Huge amounts of energy and authority are expended to keep order. Worse still, a torpid conservatism sets in, so that even positive change, such as an amalgamation or transfer of function that avoids a duplication, becomes difficult or impossible to achieve.

Indeed, turf imperatives always increase duplication of effort within an organization. Duplication may result from poor organizational design – giving the same task to two units – or from organizational expansion. Some units are blind to what goes on in more distant ones, or think they can do a job better, and so take on duties already being done somewhere else. The fuzzy boundaries between one unit's tasks and another's may actually be encouraged or exploited for reasons of turf, since it may give a unit an opportunity or an excuse to occupy someone else's turf. The competition may be purely defensive; a unit may find it necessary, as Hobbes suggested, to make conquests of its own in order to ensure that some other unit will not occupy its turf.

Duplication is a particularly serious problem among (as opposed to within) departments of government. Deputy ministers, while they hold their chairs, are feudal lords in their own right and there is little authority over them, apart from that exercised by the central core of government headed by the prime minister. However, the prime minister and his chief advisers have far too much on their plates to intervene in any but the most obvious and serious cases. Massé's venture to eliminate duplication between levels of government, and within the federal government is a worthy one and has been pressed through Programme Review to a degree that has surprised and impressed me, but it still seems only to scratch the surface, turning up high-profile cases of duplication and missing the majority of them hidden under the bureaucratic shell. Nearly any public servant could tell you horror stories of interdepartmental competition and duplication.

Turf can mean mandate, budget, or human resources. It may also mean knowledge; indeed, increasingly it is knowledge that is the most important commodity of which an organization holds possession. A government organization's services involve in a large proportion of cases provision of information. A huge number, probably the majority, of public servants should be classified as "knowledge workers," in Peter Drucker's apt phrase. Knowledge is power. It enables the larger organization to make informed decisions, provide better service and play the interdepartmental game more handily. A unit receives plaudits as its knowledge flows upstairs. Knowledge may be exchanged reciprocally with other organizations or departments. But, since it is so valuable, it may be protected, even withheld, allowed to lie unused like oil in the ground. Box organizations enclose their knowledge within walls and dispense it as appropriate, in something like an intravenous drip. "Security" may be the reason given for protecting this information, though security considerations turn out to be relevant in only a relatively small percentage of cases. Defense of knowledge-turf is, of course, small-mindedness with a vengeance. The overall quality of government service would be magnified immensely if knowledge was more freely available throughout the bureaucracy, but the system of stacked boxes is bound to make the dissemination process harder and more costly. By the same token, organizations trust only their own "knowledge" and distrust that of other bodies; they therefore erect massive information collection functions that perform the same job being done elsewhere in government.

"Control" is an important term, but many, even many within government, do not know what it means. In fact it is highly ambiguous. Frequently, it is confused with direction or planning, or even control in the crude sense of "keeping control," which is really a matter of turf or autocratic management. In financial terms, control tends to mean spending all, but not more than all, of your budget – to be sure, on prescribed or permissible activities, but this does not necessarily ensure its judicious use. A simple formula was put to me by a boss of mine some years ago. It satisfactorily defines control as a function of management. Planning is designing the work to be done. Organizing is marshalling the resources to do it and launching it. Control is checking back to make sure it gets done on schedule and to make any adjustments needed along the way.

Control may also be intimately connected with accountability, another ambiguous term. A manager, or any employee, is accountable for certain work entrusted to him or her. As projects, organizations, and budgets become bigger and more complex, outside bodies, auditors, and financial administrators of various kinds, become the agents of control, or of holding managers accountable. Control tends to take on the sense of ensuring compliance with administrative or financial rules or with the law itself. This is seen as an essential part of government, which is accountable for the judicious expenditure of public funds to Parliament.

Control as practised by management is uneven: some managers are better at it than others, but most are amateurs. Indeed, as a means of improving efficiency and effectiveness, of adjusting activities to ensure they achieve their objectives, control is a haphazard art. Few have defined standards against which success in control of work, or the achievement of results in general, should be judged. When control becomes the task of units outside the line organization, whether specialists in keeping track of expenditures, or formal audit and review organizations, expertise in control increases but the results are worse. Such units inevitably define the rules that have to be met in ever more convoluted ways. By the law of serving number one, this has the effect, if not always the explicit purpose, of giving themselves tons of work, power, and authority. They become police forces determined to find and punish wrongdoing, not service organizations facilitating solutions in operational units (illustrating the corollary of the law).

In so doing, they lose sight of the objective of control (if anyone was ever clear on it in the first place). The objective of control is undeniably to make sure monies are spent for authorized ends, but also surely to improve work by reviewing it, dealing with problems that have arisen, and making adjustments. It is to save time, energy, and money – in short, to increase efficiency. But the elaborate mechanisms of control as they have evolved do the opposite. They throw wrenches into the works, bring about protracted disputes about trivial matters, and focus heavily on compliance with rules for its own sake.

When Vice President Albert Gore announced the results of the first phase of the National Performance Review, he drew attention to the plethora of rules governing the distribution of appropriate types of ashtrays.[2] Quoting from a regulation about "ash receivers, tobacco (desk type)," the report discusses the nine pages of regulations that specify, among other things, the size, colour, polish, and sturdiness of ordinary glass ashtrays, the number, position, level, and the slope of the cigarette rests on them, and the tests they must undergo. "The specimen should break into a small number of irregular shaped pieces not greater in number than 35, and it must not dice." Such outrages are the tip of a very large, if usually less dramatic, iceberg.

The world of administration is full of highly detailed and often irrational rules – when you can claim a lunch when you are on travel status – that cost more to enforce than they save in uncovering unauthorized expenditures. Control mechanisms waste money by consuming funds needed to impose control and by interfering in work processes. Worse still, they interfere with managers by second-guessing their decisions, assuming managerial authority for themselves.

Unfortunately, spokespersons for the public interest in Parliament and in the media tend to reinforce these tendencies in their very pursuit of the integrity of the public purse. Instead of promoting cost-effectiveness, they tend to look for scandal or anomaly. By smoking out embarrassing examples, they cause managers to impose yet more layers of control or oversight, or have their organizations spend still more of their resources on defending themselves against such attack. And they punish those whose error, inadvertent or not, caused the brouhaha. The effort to encourage managers to take more risks goes out the window because of intolerance for error.

The annual budgetary cycle is seen as essential for maintaining Parliamentary control. A recent "scandal" that reached the headlines castigated a semi-independent agency and several departments for concealing multi-year expenditures in contracts with the agency. A scam? It is reasonable to assume that it was a means of avoiding a loss of funds that could not otherwise be spent and therefore of maximizing cash. But the fact is the annual budgetary cycle is a stupid straitjacket. No one doubts Parliament's need to know annually where the people's money is, but annual budgeting reduces or eliminates efficiencies that may be gained from longer-term budgeting.[3] In recognition of this, Sweden, a democracy par excellence, has adopted biannual budgetary cycles.

The auditor-general of Canada, great and venerable as this institution is, and essential to the national life, is a good example of how control and accountability at the highest level of government may work. Journalists and opposition members of Parliament rush to his annual report to see what dirt has been dug up and feature it in headlines and speeches. Managers scurry to find cover, erect defences or build new mechanisms of control to prove that they are doing something about the mess that has been uncovered. Alternatively and more calculatingly, they raise their hackles and their sabres with such gusto as to scare off the auditor-general, and everyone else. Lost in the melee is whatever constructive measures in the report might actually bring efficiency and savings to government and better service to the public.

The tangle of government administration is fully evident in budget and personnel management. I have dealt a little with both subjects along the way.

Despite "reforms" like zero-based budgeting and single operating budgets, budgets remain only partially under the control of managers.[4] Financial administrators continue to exert power, in the name of control but usually with the effect of straitjacketing and second-guessing the manager. Units strive to obtain new money or, given current tight circumstances, at least keep what they have. No unit would ever give up resources voluntarily. This may be called the law of conservation of resources. Using up most of the money in one's budget is the mark of successful budgetary management. Such units "prove" their budget forecasts were accurate and are accordingly rewarded by keeping about the same amount of money the next fiscal year. If they spend too little, they may be punished by having their "reference levels" reduced. This was what the Mulroney Government regarded as hard-nosed, effective, economical financial control and it is widely practised today, especially in Washington.

The last is the key point. Governments serious about cost-cutting should reward those units and managers able to deliver the maximum programme for minimum costs, either by letting them keep some of the amounts saved, provided they can justify effective use of these funds (as the Australians are doing), or, perhaps better, by providing their personnel with a financial bonus to be paid out of the money saved. I accept here, rather reluctantly, the argument that managers need "incentives" to save money, implying that saving the Canadian taxpayer's huge burden is not enough. This is a remedy, not a diagnosis, and I will be turning to remedies later. I raise it here to illustrate an important principle. Current government policy reinforces bad habits: it does not encourage managers to reduce their expenditures.[5]

Personnel policy in government, which at the federal level is the business of the Public Service Commission and Treasury Board, is the last main area I will discuss. It rounds out a picture of incredible, self-inflicted rigidity and labyrinthine entanglement.

Government personnel policy nourishes hierarchical values by investing tremendous resources in a multigrade, multicategory personnel classification system and in elaborate systems for appraisal and promotion. Sometimes we hear about simplification of the system – simplification is the main ideology of personnel planners today – but change is glacial and resistance strong. In many parts of the federal Public Service, there may be as many as eight grades at the support level, five or six at the officer level, and five more in executive categories, not counting the deputy minister grades. Some argue that having many grades gives people the satisfaction of having many chances at promotion. This is said to be good for morale, but it is an illusion.

Not only the people but all the positions are classified. Classifying a position is an exercise in drudgery, usually involving incomprehensible paperwork and a mysterious approval process. Knowing the game may help a manager to raise the prestige of his unit by obtaining higher classifications for his personnel, although this may not be in the interest of the organization as a whole or be financially sound. "Classification creep" is a significant source of higher personnel costs. Competitions for promotion are likewise huge efforts, heavy with committee work and paperwork, slow and daunting. Competitions to level, that is, a generalized promotion process in which everyone eligible in a certain grade is considered for the next grade, are more economical; they get the torture over at one go. Competitions for position, which are for appointments to individual jobs, are deadly: the same meticulous, burdensome effort is required time after time when vacancies occur. Appointment to level has the advantage that filling jobs is merely an administrative decision, usually a matter of short, sharp haggling between personnel officers and managers.

Fairness is supposed to be the driving force behind the promotional system. No leaf is left unturned to ensure that every eligible candidate is given his fair shot at advancement. I believe that there is an honest effort to make the system fair, but I cannot tell if it really is. When you try to impose a massive, highly detailed regime on everyone, the scope for arbitrariness is enormous – and it gets greater the smaller the room for advancement. Someone, somewhere, must make the judgement as to whose merits exceed other people's merits and the basis may be far from objective, however much "objective" data is accumulated in the form of reports and ratings. The system is burdensome and costly and less and less justified in shrinking governmental organizations. While fairness is the rule, the real motivator is usually caution. So frightened are personnel administrators of grievances and court cases, which are increasing, that they apply layers and layers of bureaucracy in the superstitious belief that these will fend off the devil. I have heard of a case in which forty hours of work were required for a competition for one position in which there was only one candidate.

A personnel department is essentially an internal service organization, but once again in accordance with the law of serving number one first, it normally becomes a barony unto itself, with its own interests and powers. Whereas a manager wants the best possible people for his staff, personnel officers have pegs that need to be jammed into holes, regardless of how good the fit is. Only within these parameters do they provide the manager with the service he wants. Personnel, moreover, is excessively and obsessively rule-driven and rule-concocting. It often develops adversarial poses toward work units, delaying or obstructing their acquisition of human resources needed for their service to real customers outside the organization, just so that it can have its own way.

Few feel empowered to transform these situations. They point upward to the Public Service Commission or Treasury Board as imposing restraints they can do nothing about. These are obstacles, to be sure, but blaming them is also a very convenient rationalization.

CHAPTER THREE

ORGANIZATION MEN

People shape organizations and are shaped by them. It may be instructive to look at it from a more personal angle. What is seen as good performance? What types thrive in the bureaucratic environment? What bad ones are encouraged by its main characteristics? I do not intend this discussion as by any means a thorough catalogue of traits; on the contrary, it may overemphasize a minority of public servants. Whether this may be seen as "unbalanced" does not greatly concern me. What seems to me important about these minorities is the extent to which they are products of the bureaucratic system and the extent to which they set a tone that helps colour the whole scene.

Before beginning, permit me a few short remarks.

First, contrary to appearences, the title of this chaper is not intened to be sexist. The justice in such a gender-specific title, other than in its vague allusiveness, lies in the fact that men on the whole created our bureaucracy. They dominated managerial hierarchies during the era of Creation almost totally, even more than they do today.

Secondly – and I repeat myself – nothing in the last chapter or this one should be taken as an attack on the integrity, ability or dedication of the vast majority of public servants or public service managers. I have known many public servants who work hard – often to the point of overwork – who meet or exceed the standards set for them, who are honest, who are intelligent, and who are highly skilled at what they do. Although the appellation should be used sparingly, there are highly talented, even brilliant, people at the apex of the Public Service, the equals of senior executives in the private sector and top administrators of other organizations. Canada has been justly praised for having among the best civil servants in the world, all the more reason to consider the failings of the Public Service structural, not the fault of individuals here or there. Moreover, quite a number of people inside government see that things have gone awry, often with great insight and systematic understanding, and are making serious efforts to change practices. What is daunting to individuals in the Public Service is the sheer immensity of the task of turning so gargantuan a ship in a different direction. Thus, many do not try

– they "do their jobs" – and many ambitious efforts, such as the Nielsen report and Public Service 2000, peter out before they have much impact, or they create more confusion than reform.

The only "sin" of many of these people is that they live and work – and succeed – within a structure that has outlived its time and has become a burden to the people it is supposed to serve. Moreover, Hobbes' law continues to apply: where individuals do have harmful influence in the public service, the bullies, the expansionists, the obsessive control hounds, and so on, they put everyone on the defensive and have an influence that outweighs their numbers.

Since the 1920s or 1930s, when patriarchs O.D. Skelton and W.C. Clark flourished, a handful of exceedingly able public servants have built up the federal bureaucracy, staffed it with talented officials – think of Lester B. Pearson and Norman Robertson – and created a legacy that, somewhat battered and bruised, still survives. The model senior official was hard-working and dedicated. He was a person of high intelligence, frequently recruited from a university. He was scrupulously fair. I do not use any of these terms lightly.

Dedication seems to me something of a distinguishing mark of people of that era both on campuses and in government, perhaps because of the influence of service-oriented religion on their upbringing. Many of its members had a sense of mission. To be sure, they were often rather colourless; they ran a big machine and ran it with skill and consistency. There was an amazing degree of consensus among the members of this elite and considerable harmony between them and the (usually) Liberal politicians of the time. This is not to say they were plodders: they were the creators, after all, of a bureaucratic system that survives stubbornly into the present. At critical times, they helped to change the orientation of this bureaucracy radically to serve new priorities, such as national unity.

Some of their spiritual descendants are still to be seen, moderate, industrious, fiercely strong believers in the ideal of public service, sound of judgment, adept at making the machine, or rather the stacks of boxes, produce as well as such things can produce. However, today's highflyer more often has different distinguishing marks. He or she is likely to be younger, frequently under fifty, as the bureaucracy, since it started to take a beating in the Trudeau years and since its mishandling by the Mulroney administration, is a tougher, harder-hitting place in which the *éminence grise* finds it more difficult to compete and survive. Stamina is essential, often even youth. "Dedication" does not seem so apt a word for the 1980s and 1990s: "ambition" – industry even to the point of workaholism and obsession – seems more apt. Some highflyers are highly innovative and creative, though there is cause for doubt as to whether these are adequate characterizations of the class as a whole. Management training classes talk-up innovation and risk-taking constantly, but a senior official walks on a tightrope. Balance is essential and caution paramount. Ministers are interested in risk-takers only when their gambles pay off. Finally, bureaucratic politics during the Mulroney years became more machiavellian. People, very senior people, were treated harshly. The political yardstick was used more often and less adroitly, both in judging personnel and in the making of appointments. Although patronage always exists in government, my impression is that it reached a new peak during the last Tory administration.

Highflyers have to be heavy hitters. Because of the expansion of the bureaucracy, enormous energy is required to cut through the crap, if you will forgive the term. People destined for the top usually earn a reputation for being able to do this early on, that is, use skill and headbanging as liberally as is needed to force action out of the stacked boxes. When they reach the top, assistant deputy minister and up, their relations with their peers can be very stormy indeed and they must be aggressive and thick-skinned to survive. One hears of (and sometimes hears) terrible shouting matches over the phone or in the meeting room. Perhaps this has always been the case and I was too far from the corridors of power to observe such unseemliness in the older generation, but at least the image of the Pearsons and Robertsons is one of greater civility and consensus.

As indicated, the key environmental factor in the emergence of this breed is the growth of the bureaucracy. Deputy ministers today are immensely powerful figures responsible for huge departments containing thousands upon thousands of staff. Departments are bigger in mass but also cover a wider range of responsibilities and have more levels. Elitists though the earlier generations were, none were leaders of such huge organizations, nor were they so distant from the bottom ranks of officers as is the case today.

A very important implication of this growth is its effect on the flow of information. The knowledge in organizations is distributed – divided – more widely and is located farther from the top level than was once the case. Senior officials are usually very bright, knowledgeable people, but they cannot know everything in all the grey cells of all the boxes of their organizations. They may think they can, not only because arrogance is liberally distributed among some of them, but because they were once themselves super desk officers who in their own right had highly detailed knowledge about some subjects.

They also tend to equate important or pertinent knowledge with the things uniquely to be learned at their level, that is, by talking to one another. Who in the bowels of their departments, after all, could aspire to the gems they pick up from daily contact with ministers and the most powerful public servants in the land? That this may produce error or distortion they sometimes realize, sometimes they do not. In any case, they are bound to recognize that they can never do without the mundane facts their subordinates sit on. They have to find ways of gaining access to them. The difficulty of having the right facts at their disposal at the right times has been discussed in the preceding chapter. Their need for these services, their impatience, the fact that they are themselves highly motivated people – "proactive" is the neologism – often exacerbate their frustration. They resort, sometimes, to the phenomenon of "government by shouting" and "management by yelling and telling" as one observer calls it.[1] A show of temper is seen as one way to wake the poor dullards up who do not know how to please them, or a threat of sanctions.

They also resort to personal sources: kitchen cabinets, people they know (who may not be the ones with the knowledge they require), their own heads. This may or may not produce better insights than the vast, dull bureaucracy can provide, but what it inevitably does is create a wider abyss between the perceptions of the world at the top and those in the middle or bottom of the chain. Vertical elites are created in the organization, units or lines of command more trusted than others. Duplication of services often occurs. Given the amount of knowledge or information in the organization that does not reach the top, it is impossible for all major decisions to be well-informed. A substantial number may fall into this category. Inevitably, the top-heavy nature of the organization has significant impact on the attitudes and performance of those down below.

Clique formation affects personnel policy. In the olden days, nearly everyone knew nearly everyone else. Personal connections were therefore of undoubted importance but they were of a different order, the connections of members of a fairly small club. Merit, at the same time, seems to have kept its meaning. This is less true today, despite the heavy, impersonal, methodical fairness of personnel systems. The top people are much more likely to use personal connections – patron-client ties – to ensure they have trusted supporters within their organizations; they have handsome rewards to dispense and they are adept at spotting talent and helicoptering its possessors through the ranks at a dizzying pace. Since the members of an elite are not always sound judges, the result from time to time is that some people who end up at the heights are the wrong ones, less qualified than many of their erstwhile peers. This is sometimes a cause of resentment, and a fast-riser has to be very good indeed to survive when his protector departs from the scene. Incidentally, another increasing phenomenon is the intervention of ministers in public service appointments. Flagrant as this was during the Mulroney years, it seems just as prominent today.

In the eyes of their suboridinates, highflyers can do no wrong. They demand loyalty. Their initiatives are acts of genius. There is a degree of openness before a decision is made. Afterward, no one may cavil, whine or question from the sidelines at peril of beetle-browed glares and eventual sanctions. (High-flyers can be quite ruthless.) The successful people in the chain of command are not just yes-men, but *enthusiastic* yes-men. They make the initiative work, and if it does not but does not fail too badly, they will cover up the fact. Proofs can always be trotted out to show things in their "proper" light. Almost no performance standards are set in advance against which the initiative can be honestly and fairly tested. The boss, middle managers, and practically everyone else has a stake in hiding mistakes and errors because they are equated with failure.

Highflyers may demand and reward creativity and brilliance, and talk-up risk-taking and empowerment, but their commitment to these things seems to me rather doubtful. What they often mean by initiative is anticipation: it is much nicer to have a subordinate who meets your need without having to be told. Moreover, senior officials rarely let power slip from their hands to any significant extent. At least two reasons exist for this. One is organizational: today's senior officials may be a different breed from their forerunners but they still operate within traditional bureaucratic forms, and I would suggest, are substantially committed to them. They live or die by satisfying their ministers. Secondly, by another, more personal application of the law of serving number one, they are not interested in change that would reduce their own power. They may justify this to themselves by arguing that, after all, they are the best of the lot, so why should they trust the judgment and the actions of inferior talent.

Small wonder there is such poor morale in bureaucracies today! Poor morale is often put down to job instability and budget cuts and these are indeed potent factors. But I have observed the phenomenon for years, starting long before Programme Review and shrinkage appeared on the scene. Poor morale is an inevitable consequence of bureaucratic structure. Middle-ranking and junior officials by and large are, to coin a phrase, forgotten people at the bottom of the bureaucratic pyramid. The weight of hierarchy above them, the very limited scope they are given for action and decision, the tight leash on which they are held, all combine to rob them of any sense that they are doing anything of value. They are supposed to be happy cogs. The ideology of traditional public service is built around persuading people that cogs can be happy, just as the ideology of private sector organizations traditionally demanded of little people that they prize being little and mean and just doing their job.

Formally, decisions of state are made by ministers, but masses of important decisions are delegated to the bureaucracy. Decision-making within the bureaucracy is very much the prerogative of the most senior levels; it without question sits at the top of the hierarchy and any attempt to delegate it downwards tends to be of temporary effect. Decision-making, as if on an invisible elastic band, keeps recoiling back up.

What are some of the traits and values of middle managers? What turns them on? What do they see as a mark of distinction? What do they, or their superiors, consider the things that will help them get ahead?

One is the size and value of their turf. Just as the size of one's land holdings was the source of prestige and status for the leisure classes of nineteenth century Europe, the size of a unit, its budget, the importance of its responsibilities and the information it possesses are powerful sources of prestige for a manager. Under the laws of maximization and integrity of turf, and of the conservation (if not expansion) of resources, managers adopt the values of acquisition, or at least preservation of power and "wealth."

They are usually lionized if they are successful in obtaining new money. The old game, beginning in about the 1970s when growth was the rule, was a matter of creating a convincing enough argument for the need for a higher budget. A good case usually won a satisfactory reward. Now, an executive is considered especially proficient if he is able to keep or expand his pot of money in hard times when all about him others are losing their pants. No one ever thinks of giving up resources voluntarily. If he does he is considered a great fool. Spending most of the money in one's budget is the mark of successful budgetary management.

Managers are expected to serve their superiors. This may be manifested in flooding the senior levels with information so as to avoid being caught out when a specific need arises. It usually shows itself in caution, often excessive caution, to ensure that the quality of product being sent upstairs is "perfect" or, under the law of the conservation of resources, to protect knowledge and information for as long as possible until they can be pulled from a hat and have their maximum impact.

Just as knowledge in the hands of decision-makers may be inadequate or be based on too few sources, the information that comes from below may be inadequately shaped or focused to facilitate the best-informed decision. Not only do middle managers lack the perspective of the top, which may not have been well communicated to them through the maze of levels; they may not feel responsible for the ultimate decision, given that power and authority reside so far away, in another country, so to speak. The stake of the middle or junior manager is diminished and buck-passing or fence-sitting may be the result. "It wasn't my decision," is a common excuse, or,

"I will just wait and see which way the wind is blowing." Procrastination tends to be encouraged. A hard problem in one's in-basket may go away if you leave it long enough. "There! I knew if I ignored it that it would resolve itself," I have heard frequently enough – even from my own lips. This is not very praiseworthy, but neither is it very unreasonable. Since authority and responsibility are continually being pressed upward, why should low-level managers risk their necks? Moreover, since the bureaucracy is so large and events in the real world move so rapidly, some problems really do go away or change before a bureaucrat can deal with them. But others do not and the manager's procrastination does nothing to resolve them.

Unless the managers have great energy, moreover, they will have little time left for customers. Since the eyes of managers are usually directed upwards where power and authority lie, their focus on customers suffers.

As it is very important to middle managers to look good, they focus on success stories. But mechanisms to identify problem areas and improve them are generally weak in the Public Service, though a conscientious manager will see them, work at them and seek outside help if he needs it. As noted above, middle managers must also make their bosses look good. Nay-sayers, critical thinkers, anyone who pierces the balloon of Public Service achievement, becomes a cynic, a rebel, an "off the wall" type. (To make matters worse, some of them are.)

One last remark: it is well known in the Public Service – one is reminded of the Peter Principle – that many people obtain promotion to managerial ranks because of their success as desk officers. Some of these never learn the management game: delegation, allocating work, monitoring, controlling. They behave as "super-desk" officers. They are the repositories of all knowledge and wisdom in their units. The staff are their scribes. I have known managers who, far from giving direction, actually dictated written work they wanted junior officers to prepare. A charismatic leader may motivate his staff not only to support him but to be productive and innovative as well. The impact of the dominant, know-it-all leader is harmful. Work is overcentralized, decision-making slowed (since everything depends on the boss), staff rendered useless (secretaries would do) and morale undermined. The development of staff in these circumstances is frozen. People stop believing in themselves.

Bullies in the Public Service deserve a brief mention of their own. We all know too well what bullies are, but in the Public Service they have their own particular characteristics. Bullies tend to be out for themselves. They like power. They like to beat up on others, making no exceptions for the weak. They enjoy status and command. If they are able, their organizations may be relatively effective, especially if staff can be cajoled into support for their boss's objectives: this type of bully is also a leader. Bullies tend to be heavy-hitters and so may be effective in forcing action out of other organizations. On the whole, though, they tend to be bad for morale, uncooperative, and ultimately, bad for an organization's effectiveness and the effectiveness of the larger organization of which it is a part. An overt bully who is constantly throwing his weight around may intimidate his way upward for a time, but usually creates enough distrust and discomfort to undo himself in the end. His judgment may be skewed. His power and control are normally more important to him than doing what is best. Reasonable people will stand for only so much.

I have referred to the phenomenon of expansionism. Both this and its mirror image, excessive, almost paranoid defensiveness, cause no end of anxiety within bureaucracies and lead to the creation or maintenance of duplication. When a bully achieves a position of power, he espies a role that really belongs to another organization. He decides to erect a whole new edifice to assume that role. His action wastefully duplicates what others are doing, but he will fight tooth and nail to achieve his ends as though his very life depended on it. Or major changes in some area of government operations massively alter the terrain, putting some unit effectively out of business. The bully in charge may never admit that the change has taken place, or may seek arguments – there will always be arguments just as for Dylan Thomas there will always be uncles – to defend keeping the resources and perhaps even the function. This happens over and over again. The result is many dead branches on the bureaucratic tree.

Bullies tend to be insecure. They do not cooperate readily with others. Indeed, they may be downright incapable of cooperation. They like their boxes to be black boxes. They may have a neurotic obsession with control of their own units. Although they are far from the only ones to do so – a disposition to fictionalize is shared by all types – they go to extremes to accentuate the positive. They become determined to hide their operations to outsiders and always put the best possible face on them, regardless of the facts. They become "good news" junkies. They focus on success stories almost to the point of suppressing any report of failure or problem. If they get away with it, their units become impervious to outside scrutiny. They may justify such subterfuge as being in the best interest of staff morale. This is nonsense. Their approach produces either complacency or large-scale cynicism. Why do they behave in this way? Because for them the truth is of very little value compared with their own power.

Autocratic within and defensive without, they are unable to share responsibility or delegate it to others. They terrorize their staff into submission. "Shut up and do what you are told!" Ostensibly welcoming opinions, they reply to thoughtful but unorthodox comment, "No, that is absolutely wrong." They sometimes fail in the end simply because the tasks get too onerous for them to keep on top of them by themselves. Moreover, the shield of secrecy becomes so opaque that it becomes difficult for anyone outside to tell whether they are doing well or not. Something may go very much astray and someone may blow the whistle. The "black box syndrome" may then become unacceptable to their superiors. The amazing thing, though, is that bullies are often able to get away with their behaviour for long periods and may even be considered effective managers much of the time.

It was noted in discussing hierarchy that one of the elements that exists in chicken-and-egg symbiosis with it is the belief that supervisory experience is necessary in order to get promoted. In the Public Service, the ambition of probably the majority of officers is to become managers. Promotion to managerial ranks is a sign of success and lack of promotion failure. However, as the upper ranks have thinned during the age of restraint and the opportunities for promotion decreased, the sub-managerial ranks are filled with too many nestlings seeking too few worms. A sense of failure, depression, and paralysis predominate. Salvation lies in the still more desperate effort to obtain supervisory experience at the sub-managerial level, as deputy director, section head or even desk head, all to nourish the faint hope of advancement.

The hunger to supervise is seen as justified, but is it? Those inside organizations see the value of a ranks-and-orders "culture" as self-evident. In fact, there is nothing self-evident about it. It reminds us of Hobbes' reduction of the basic values of "natural" man, more or less, to covetousness and envy.[2] Although the hierarchical model traditionally dominated the private sector as well as the public sector, and still does in many companies, it has been displaced in many others. Cooperation, teamwork, quality of service, and expanded responsibility at lower levels are transforming bureaucratic values. Defining workers' worth by their place on the ladder is bound to fade in such organizations either because there is no ladder, or because it has become truncated.

The military provides us with a working model of an organization built thoroughly around rank. Those on the inside know nothing else, and solidarity demands that everyone view privilege as the prerogative of level. Anyone who dissents is considered insubordinate and dealt with harshly. In fact, in the military there is some justification for this point of view, in that those higher in rank need the authority to command those lower down to take actions that put their lives at risk. Giving this factor its due, one can even admire, in the abstract, some aspects of this way of life, certainly the courage, and sometimes the order and discipline. But hierarchy, though widely influential and almost universally imitated, is arguably, indeed increasingly, inappropriate for bureaucratic organizations. In personal life, it can also be unattractive to the point of being ugly or absurd. We have all seen how ridiculous a military man may become when he tries to apply the values of his profession outside their proper context: obsessions about haircuts, treating one's children like subalterns, and the like.

For most people, there is no compelling reason to adopt the hierarchical model. From a moral point of view, obtaining personal satisfaction from one's place on the ladder, from the enjoyment of power, and from the envy of others, is not very commendable. It is a ripe target for satire. Some would claim that such values are natural to humanity, but although there is no doubt something in this, humanity's values may be getting confused with particular kinds of institutional values. Surely it is at least as natural to cherish the pleasure of one's own work, teamwork, and the exercise of knowledge and skills. Moreover, it is reasonable to expect that one should be financially rewarded for expertise, effectiveness, and the quality of one's work, not simply for one's position. One needs to judge practices on the basis of their results, not on any alleged fit with human nature. Hierarchy is innately inefficient, slow, expensive, and self-serving. It demonstrates the principle, the more hands, the more error.

The majority of public servants, and especially Public Service managers, tend, whether actively or tacitly, to support existing organizational practices. This is far from an earthshaking observation. Organizations are run by rules and they train their people in these rules. Personnel are expected to promote their organizations and it is natural for most to defend their rules and basic principles. A pervasive characteristic of the bureaucracy and the people in it is self-praise and cover-up. Units do not want to be judged by others. They want to keep the power of appraisal in their own hands, so that practically all appraisal is self-appraisal. But their judgments are suspect, first because they are self-serving (the law of number one again) and secondly because very few independent means exist to judge the bureaucracy or its personnel honestly. Sometimes the process is consciously cynical: "information" is planted so as to lead to a predetermined conclusion. More often, bureaucrats think they are being objective, but try as they might, the play of interests in an organization skews facts and information till they are unrecognizable. In any case, integrity can be dangerous. Incisive critics become "bad-mouthers" and negators. Many save their criticism for the cafeteria or the coffee break. Small wonder that reform sufficient to make a significant difference is unlikely to come from within government bureaucracy.

This is a depressing picture. But, if any of it is right, what is to be done? We need to turn the page and begin to think about the cure.

CHAPTER FOUR

THE ROLE OF GOVERNMENT

Society can no longer afford government as costly as our levels of government have become. Even cut back, governments must perform much more efficiently than they have performed before. Reform of the public sector is largely a matter of narrowing the role of government and redesigning its processes. What games can government get out of altogether? What games can be reinvented? And how can it play better at games it will continue to have to play?

Merely cutting, "using the axe," is a poor, indeed a discredited, means of solving the problem of the size of government and its debt. Yet, it has been the preferred instrument of governments to meet deficit-cutting targets. Annual across-the-board cuts, wage freezes, staff reductions, paring programmes here and there have become routine. A more radical version of this approach is proposed by right-wing populism – Reform in Canada and the Republicans in the U.S. – which call for far more massive cuts, including wholesale slashing of social security programmes, to create surpluses that can begin to pay off the national debt.

One bit of proof that the axe by itself is ineffective is that, at federal and provincial levels, the annual deficit has, by and large, continued its upward trend despite these measures. There are some well known reasons for this. The recession brought with it huge increases in transfers, such as unemployment insurance, and the swelling of provincial welfare rolls. The growing national debt inevitably means that interest payments have grown even in periods when interest rates have come down. Politicians have been notoriously unwilling both to make the hard decisions and to stick with them. We the electors have not helped: we keep demanding more benefits for which we are unwilling or unable to pay. In addition, confusion and resistance within the bureaucracies tend to delay or diminish the full realization of savings. With their massive protective layering built up over so many years, they are adept at deflecting attacks or delaying their effects. Despite cuts, many units still manage to expand.

But these are not the only reasons, or even the most important, why the axe alone is a poor instrument. Budget cuts can only be effective when they are combined with a coherent strategy, a clear vision of the role we want government to have and the way we want it to do its business. Some managers may apply a cut by dropping unnecessary or duplicated activities, but most apply such cuts relatively indiscriminately – "across the board" is the usual terminology. Priorities are not established in advance to give managers guidance as to what activities may be curtailed. A frequent complaint at the working level is that units are simply required to do more with less. This is a losing battle. Staff become overloaded. The implications of stress over the long term for physical and mental health, and for productivity, are obvious. Some work does not get done. Standards of service fall. Savings, in the form of gained efficiency, are not realized. Greater inefficiency, which is the very opposite of what leaders hoped to achieve, is the inevitable result.

The current government has recognized the shortcomings of the axe. Massé's Programme Review has begun to develop principles for more rational, priority-driven reductions. Yet, many people view Programme Review cynically as just another cover for arbitrary cuts. The finance minister's axe still seems to operate independently of principle. And his eye still roves to identify soft and vulnerable tax hits that may ease his bottom line. What is needed is a marriage of Programme Review and budget reduction. The extent to which the 1995 federal budget achieved that union is a matter of opinion; I expect that most observers consider it a far from perfect one. It established reasonably ambitious short-term budgetary reduction targets. There will be a need to adhere to them and deepen them in subsequent years. Many cuts – to transfer payments, welfare programmes and administration – were mere "salami slicing" in bureaucratic jargon. They did not flow from a clear plan that determined how savings were to be achieved. Where departments did undertake detailed reviews and produce plans that identified changes in their programmes, they did so in such haste – a matter of months – that their efficacy in many instances is open to question. The lack of focus will reveal itself in the difficulty of implementation. Moreover, the real capacity of governments, ministers and their officials, to drop programmes has yet to be tested in depth. The phenomenon of "more with less" still rules in many domains.

Programme Review does honestly address the question of what the appropriate role of government should be. Its answer is: a role that we can afford. This is a pragmatic and cost-oriented approach, and as far as it goes, it is a solid one. A second approach is moral and philosophical. The answer from this perspective will reflect our deepest values and beliefs about humanity and society, freedom and responsibility.

Defining the role of government breaks down into two interrelated questions: What should government do? What should government not do?

There is a view that redefining the role of government, in the sense of getting it out of many lines of business, is the only way to cut costs and increase efficiency. Peter Drucker, for example, advances this thesis, more or less, in *Post-Capitalist Society,* basing it on the assumption that an institution that is fundamentally rule-bound can never run anything efficiently.[1] This may be true, but I work on the hypothesis that government has little choice but to carry on some of its operations and must do them more efficiently.

We can look at the governmental functions now to be discussed as a series of concentric circles, the innermost representing the core functions of government, the outermost porous membranes that share responsibility with the non-governmental sector.

The "inner circle" of governmental functions is, first and foremost, laying down and enforcing the rules that allow people to pursue their desires in peace. They limit freedom to the extent necessary to protect the like freedom of others. No one may injure or arbitrarily limit the freedom of another member of society. Criminal law is the main vehicle for protecting the basic rights of the person. At an even more general level are the constitutional guarantees and laws protecting people against discrimination. The principal ones are the Charter of Rights and Freedoms embedded in the Constitution and the Canadian Human Rights Act, the latter being overseen by a permanent commission of the same name. Freedom of information and privacy have been the subject of still more recent legal protection. Currently, a bill on employment equity is before Parliament and similar legislation exists in some provinces.

In fact, the government's central role in law enforcement, defence, and international relations has remained unchanged since the dawn of modern political thought in the seventeenth century, indeed before. These areas, like all others, need to be run responsibly and efficiently, and like the set of "central agency" functions discussed next, they have a propensity to know no bottomline. There is always more to do and there is no clear principle that determines when enough is enough. Of course, when the security of the country is at stake, as in wartime, the case for expanding the military machine is obvious, but in normal times there have to be spending limits for these areas. The defence department has repeatedly been dealt reductions in recent years, therefore, and law enforcement and foreign affairs have also experienced cuts. Having said this, I will take government's primary role in these spheres for granted. I will have more to say about this subject, especially law enforcement, in the chapters to come.

Apart from these activities, government has a central policy function, typified by the "central agencies." In Canada they are principally the Privy Council Office, and the Department of Finance and Treasury Board. I will likewise dwell only briefly on these areas. They too are in some sense "essential," involving advice to the government on its central policies, priorities, and legislative agenda, the financing of government operations and the basic rules under which government is to conduct its business. These are core traditional government activities and the hardest to change. The pure bureaucrat thrives in them, the most adept at advising governments, the elitist, the most authoritative, the most powerful, sometimes the most brilliant, sometimes the most arrogant, sometimes the most cautious and rule-bound. They are closest to the centre of government, to ministers and the prime minister. Theirs is the world of high policy, of fiat, of management, of control, of senior appointments, of facing political flak.

It would be an understatement to say that these functions are not immune from criticism on grounds of efficiency and absurd to suggest that they should be exempt from budgetary restraint. In fact, they exemplify the textbook difficulty of measuring the usefulness and cost-effectiveness of government. They exist to serve the public interest but for them the public interest is an abstraction. They have no customers. Their orientation, their agenda, is almost exclusively upward. They live at the pinnacle of the governmental pyramid, driven wild (no one would deny that they work hard) by the insistent, and almost always very short-term, demands of all the most senior and powerful Cabinet ministers, including the prime minister himself, of high officials and of parliamentarians. Their status as servants of the public is deeply compromised, as a result, by power, distance and imperial prerogative. On resource questions, they are as self-protective, self-serving, and territorial as any other department of government. And when push comes to shove, they always have the muscle – often the prime minister's – to get what they want. The decades of the 1970s and 1980s saw a massive expansion of these central agencies, especially the Privy Council Office. Those of a certain age will recall without difficulty characterizations of the Prime Minister's Office and the Privy Council Office as Trudeau's "White House" soon after he came to power. That remains an apt description of what these bodies have remained.

But the central agencies also provide the leadership to promote affordable government in the line departments through the policies – financial policies, personnel policies, priorities – that they set or enforce. Their record in this area is very mixed, as the discussions of indebtedness, financial management, and personnel policy in earlier chapters show. The Treasury Board, for example, is at present a typical instance of muddle. It is the manager of government, wielding the axe of day-to-day restraint; it is the source of many of the most advanced and innovative views on streamlining and offloading activities (supporting thrusts, for example, on information technology, reengineering, and alternative ways for delivering government services). But it is equally the source of the most hidebound and inflexible rules on personnel management, financial control, and contracting with the private sector. A new, government-wide expenditure management system now being advanced seems to me a promising step in improving the way departments budget and spend their money. It applies many of the principles of Programme Review, seeking to instil business planning concepts, such as costing of processes, not units of government, and performance measurement. But side by side with this bold but still theoretical innovation, reports of Treasury Board suppression of other reasonable innovations continue to abound.[2] Values of control continue to predominate over the achievement of better service and economics. Personnel classification systems also remain impervious to significant change. The Treasury Board remains the ultimate defender of rank, and in consequence, of the inflexible and hierarchical work structures around which the bureaucracy is organized.

Broad-based cuts and de-layering have been the preferred means of trimming these bureaucracies, with mixed effects. Efficiency in policy-type agencies remains largely undefined and performance standards continue to be elusive.

The term "regulation" is ambiguous. There is a broad, indeed vague, concept of regulation that means something more like control or management in general. We use the term in this way when we speak of "market regulation" in contrast with "government regulation" of the economy. This expression is confused and I will avoid it altogether, referring only to management of the economy or some part of the economy. It is important to bear in mind, however, that many of the times you see the word "regulation" it is being used in this way.

In a more precise sense, regulation is setting, applying, and enforcing rules for various areas of national life, and a regulation is in fact just a rule. This usage covers law making, defining rules for applying laws (the "regulations" that are often stipulated in an act) and establishing still more detailed rules and policies within departments to carry out a legislative mandate. The expression "administrative law" is sometimes used for such things. However, I do not mean regulation in this sense either. Rather, I mean the application of a narrower set of laws or rules that we usually call standards.

"Standard," too, is ambiguous. We speak of standards in at least three ways, ways that overlap irritatingly but that are still broadly separable. There is a broad commercial application of the term. We may speak of standard light bulbs or refer to a technology, like Windows, as setting a standard most manufacturers employ. Such standards are very important in bringing down costs for the consumer and establishing a certain level of convenience or of quality in industrial products, but they do not have anything to do with government regulation (which is not to say that governments may not meddle in such things from time to time).

Standards may also define the quality of products or services, either a minimum acceptable quality or an ideal or maximum quality, as when we say that a product sets the standard for others in the field, meaning it is the best. Of itself this notion does not involve us in government regulation either. Shoddy products, ones that do not meet standards, are not necessarily illegal or subject to government control. The standards that governments are by and large interested in, and that are the meat of government regulation, are usually minimum standards of quality, namely those that must be met to ensure protection of the public interest. Toys of poor quality are subject to government regulation when they endanger the lives or the health of infants. Electrical products are substandard when they are safety hazards and so on.

Rules may also be designed to ensure fairness in some sphere of activity or even to establish its ground rules. Examples are the regulation of corporations, banks, the money supply, the labour market, and the stock market. This is regulation of a different type from, say, safety standards but it is also a quite legitimate sphere of government involvement in our lives. However, one must be clear here not to slide into the notion of regulation as management, in which government is an active player in an activity, and not merely the body responsible for its frame of reference. We are talking about making sure companies compete with one another under non-discriminatory rules that allow each of them an equal chance, based on their own efficiency, creativity and services, to capture a share of the market. Monopolies may be broken up, or less satisfactorily, made subject to government rules, to ensure against exploitation of the public. Labour regulations seek to guarantee people fair access to employment or in the event of unemployment to the appropriate remedies, and give working people full freedom of assembly to form organizations – such as unions – to represent them and defend their interests.

Other typical examples of government regulation include safety in the work place, environmental standards, standards for various products (wiring of light fixtures) and services (banking), transportation safety, standards for health and food products, and so on. A special sort of regulation, perhaps unique to Canada, is that of the Commissioner of Official Languages, who monitors the provision of services in both official languages by federal departments and agencies and deals with complaints from the public.

We can find regulatory activities at federal, provincial and municipal levels, but not all standards that serve the public interest are or need to be set by governments – there are independent public bodies like the Canadian Standards Association that set them in some areas. This model should be kept in mind as an option, even though public bodies responsible to the people through Parliament are often the preferred ones to act as neutral arbiters.

The costs and benefits of regulation need to be carefully weighed. There is strong evidence, for example, that deregulation of the air industry has had serious repercussions for airline safety. Nor has it coincided with prosperity in this troubled industry. Deregulation and tough times appear to have conspired together to increase safety risks for travellers. Whether regulation should be carried out by government, independent public bodies, non-governmental associations, or the private sector itself, should be decided assiduously against the touchstone of the public interest.

The matter does not end here, because regulatory bodies can be as troublesome as the disorder they are meant to control. Clear limitations should apply to them. Regulatory agencies, including internal control mechanisms in government, are prone to zeal-induced proliferation. Overdoing it is addictive. There is always more to be done and there are always too few people to do it, always more environment to protect and safety to be promoted. The potential for them to do more harm than good by interfering beyond their mandate (by the law of maximization of turf) is strong.

An example is heritage designation. I am a strong supporter of protecting our heritage, and critical of the mindless and soulless "development" that would destroy – and has destroyed – much of it. I also accept that there have probably been more errors on the side of legalized vandalism than on the side of persecution of innocent individuals. Nevertheless, the latter occurs too often. Every municipality has its stories of regulatory interference in people's private affairs, their management of their very homes, often simply as a result of delays in providing permits or making decisions. There are also too many absurd designations, Ottawa certainly a prime case with its "interesting example of the Chicago style," the extraordinarily ugly and dilapidated Daly Building, that eventually collapsed almost of its own accord. These long drawn-out, costly and unreasonable stands cast in doubt more valuable preservation, successful examples of which in Ottawa include the "Sussex Village" and some of the development around Confederation Square, or the survival of Old Montreal in the heart of that large city. Toronto, by contrast, a victim of rapid growth, has preserved little of its heritage.

One solution to the problem of misplaced zeal is to set a financial ceiling on these bureaucracies and force regulators to define the priority tasks that can be done within them. Another is to find ways to streamline their processes so that they provide prompt, helpful service, and behave as policemen only in the minority of cases in which there is real wrongdoing. The public is usually a client, not an adversary, and needs to be treated as such.

The core role of government in fiscal regulation is conservative, involving such things as control of the money supply and interest rate policy. Unpopular and controversial these subjects may be, but they are important because the consequences of wrong decisions can be catastrophic. Setting clear, predictable rules within which the economy as a whole must operate is and will always be a core function of effective government. The much beleaguered Bank of Canada has actually served us well in this regard.

Nevertheless, fiscal "regulation" may be a tool of policy, seeking to achieve greater equality or to sustain growth or mitigate recession. This passes over into the improper sense of "regulation" as management of an activity. For the present, I wish only to underline the importance of government's real regulatory function in establishing a simpler, more predictable, less aggressive, less discriminatory fiscal framework. Such systems do not create wealth, but if they are applied wisely, they create the conditions without which there can be no efficient production and little wealth.

Government intervention in "industries," that is, in activities of a social, cultural, and economic character, has been a common theme of twentieth century "governance." It has taken at least three forms over and above regulation:

- Creating instruments to bring public policy considerations to bear upon these activities: some spheres of activity in which these have been particularly prominent are transport, communications, cultural industries and regional development. Marketing boards, limited largely to the agricultural sector, probably belong in this category.
- Subsidization of certain activities: subsidies have been showered upon virtually every sector of national life, including agriculture, industry, and communications.
- The actual running of enterprises that operate in the marketplace. The Crown corporation, a very prominent feature of national life in Canada at both the federal and provincial level, is the familiar instrument.

This division is neat but it does not always work out in practice. Sometimes bodies that have regulatory functions, in that they lay down rules intended to ensure an activity serves an important national interest, also intervene in the operations of the activity. I will give some examples. Sometimes a mechanism for bringing public policy to bear on an area also subsidizes it. Moreover, Crown corporations, although supposedly more responsive to government policy than their private sector cousins, may themselves be subject to a layer of governmental management, often under the guise of "regulation." This rather messy reality provides a case, at the very least, for cleaning these functions up so that they have clear, simple, straightforward purposes.

With these we straddle the line between an essential government role and a dispensable one. A scalpel, or some blunter instrument, needs to pare this to a minimum, and, of course, the process has already begun. But I will do my best to leave the cutting to the next chapter.

In any case, it is not easy simply to propose cutting the whole area of government intervention. A broad principle for when it may be relevant may be stated as follows: government has a role to intervene where compelling policy reasons or the national interest demand it. Such justifications have been used frivolously in our times; they need to be tightened up considerably.

A historical example may illustrate this rule, namely wartime measures: central management of economies has been used all over the developed world to ensure that the resources needed for a war effort are squeezed out and find their way to the front. Whether there were better alternatives is hard to say: our leaders certainly envisaged none. However, one lesson we can draw from this is that it is of very limited application. It is at most applicable when national survival is at stake.

Another example was the building of the Canadian Pacific transcontinental railroad in the 1870s and 1880s. This was an enterprise in nation-building, and if Canada was an entity worth creating, as I certainly believe, its encouragement, development and funding by government was an essential, profoundly visionary act.

The argument for nation-building has been applied much more widely by nationalists and sometimes by government decision-makers. It is suggested that a totally free market pits small Canadian producers against much larger American ones. Thus, the cause of national survival prompts the adoption of policies and the creation of a host of agencies designed to skew the market in favour of Canadians. Perhaps the National Energy Policy is the most obvious recent example.

Agencies to which I cannot deny the appellation "regulatory" but whose functions go well beyond regulation are the Canadian Radio-television and Telecommunications Commission and those set up for transport industries. When the CRTC sets prices and fee structures (as in the case of the monopoly Bell Canada), its "regulatory" function is indistinguishable from management of the sector. When it lays down rules for the percentage of Canadian ownership in broadcasting, it clearly is acting in the cause of preserving national identity, national unity and independence, but it is hard for me to distinguish this from the policy-driven management of an industry. Marketing boards are very close to this model. They exist primarily to serve the interests of agricultural producers by keeping prices high and protecting them against foreign competition. In transport, the famous and just terminated Crow Rate – the artificially low rail charges set for grain on its way, principally, to markets across the Pacific – was used to make Canadian grain exports more competitive.

Although often associated with these instruments, subsidization in its pure form is simply allocating public moneys to particular sectors or enterprises. The federal government has for many years provided major funding to higher education in Canada, despite the fact that it lacks any constitutional mandate to do so. This is a reflection less of the ambition of government than of the imbalance of the tax system, which has tended to "under-resource" the provinces. The federal government has in general avoided seeking to intervene in education policy through the transfer process per se, but smaller programmes that fund academic research directly, such as those of The Canada Council and The Social Sciences and Humanities Research Council, are more intrusive. Understandably, academics rush to take advantage of these funds with little concern about academic freedom. Until recently, Industry Canada and its predecessors had far-reaching programmes to subsidize Canadian industry, especially small- and medium-sized enterprises. Investment in research and development has been a primary focus.

Spending to keep people employed may involve subsidies to private industry or it may involve more direct intervention in the economy, as it does in public works projects directly funded by governments. Doing this to maintain employment in times of recession, *à la* Keynes, is a legitimate government activity in normal times. As has been said, it is an instrument the right to which we have in large measure forfeited for the time being because of our huge deficit, and because we have kept spending all the time rather than only during downturns. Moreover, we must not expect too much out of such things. Roosevelt did not spend his way out of the Great Depression: the war accomplished that for him. Public works are of some use from time to time because they put a few people to work, restore a bit of morale, and install infrastructure that we have to go on improving and investing in anyway.

Subsidization and intervention in the market for national policy reasons are most obviously seen in the phenomenon known as "regional development." Politically, a government will not survive long if it turns its back on poverty in Newfoundland or the restive alienation of Western Canadians, but these interventions need to be reexamined from the point of view of their real effects.

The era of the Crown corporation has not ended totally, but its heyday has passed as a result of the Mulroney Government's privatization measures. Indeed, his administration deserves considerable credit for getting government out of these gold-plated forms of intervention in our economic life. I will not dwell on this, therefore. However, Crown corporations continue to survive in the provinces and the concept continues to play a central role in the politically sensitive cultural industries. CBC/Radio Canada may be seen as the archetypal Crown corporation, its role one of defining and promulgating national identity and promoting national unity. Does there continue to be a solid case for such government enterprises in broadcasting? Where is the appropriate place to draw the line between national priorities and what is economically affordable? I will try to address these issues in the next chapter.

I have noted the extent to which instruments of policy have grown complicated and confused. Although it does not quite fit, I would like to take a quick look at the tax system from this point of view, because it too is widely used as an instrument of economic policy.

Government must have efficient means to collect the taxes that pay for its activities. But our tax system has become horrendously overloaded with functions and objectives other than this one, including fiscal policy, income redistribution, and encouragement of economic activity. Tax reform in the late 1980s simplified the system a little, but it remains a colossal mess. What is needed is a set of tax rules that are clear, simple, and fair.

Is our tax system fair? A fair system would consist of simple, stable rules that create predictability for taxpayers. Our system fails on many counts. The rules fluctuate annually, even semi-annually, making prediction hazardous. It has too many provisions with too many objectives. Some provisions are designed to help the poor ("progressive" taxation, special exemptions, and so on); some can only be exploited for real gain by the rich (measures concerning capital gains and losses, the dividend tax credit); and others assault the middle class (surtaxes, clawbacks). A fair system would never have hesitated so long in imposing a minimum tax – has it been achieved in practice even now? It is appalling that many of those who are richest and gain the greatest economic benefits from society should be able to work tax loopholes (concerning capital losses and the like) to pay no taxes. On the other hand, fairness would usually imply that everyone pay the same share of his or her income in tax. Because the principle of progressive taxation – increasing the rate of tax with increased income – is so profoundly established in the twentieth century, it is never questioned. It is a modern dogma.

Fairness is doubly hard to achieve because the concept harbours a troublesome ambiguity. It means not only establishing logical, predictable rules that treat everyone alike; it is also about redistributing income, pursuing greater material equality. When finance ministers say that they want to "close loopholes," they may have equal treatment in mind. A tax rule that allows someone a special advantage is not fair and should be eliminated, unless there is some *very* good reason for keeping it. (The trouble is that these "very good reasons" become so numerous, so convoluted, so indiscriminate, so responsive to disparate lobbies and interests, and so contradictory that they probably serve us worse than we would be served by simply not accepting most reasons as good.) But I cannot be persuaded that they mean only this. They often have in mind greater income equality, though that may mask a simple desire to squeeze more out of middle and upper income groups. Anything becomes fair that serves that end – and anything that does not becomes a "loophole." This overloading of the term "fairness" is partly the result of confusion and partly the influence of modern political ideology but it is politically clever too. By appealing to a principle none of us disavow without appearing to be scoundrels, they obtain legitimacy for a tax grab. And by promising to take more from higher than from lower income groups, they play to the understandable desire of the latter to see more of the nation's wealth transferred to them.

Obviously, there is a real need to sort out these conflicting aims and pursue them in more straightforward ways. The taxation system should be redesigned to fulfill its one principal objective: collect revenue in an equitable manner.

Insofar as the preceding section deals with income redistribution, it introduces the area of social policy, to which I shall now turn. Social security really consists of two major parts: the net designed to catch the needy and universal schemes whose benefits we all share. Although not always seen so, especially on the right, the first is surely an essential task of government; the second is often desirable and now so much a part of our lives that we assume its indispensability. Both areas, however, have been undergoing adjustment for some time, especially the latter, and are in need of further large-scale revamping, because of inefficiencies, duplication, poor rationale in some instances, and high costs. As I write, the salvoes in the Axworthy campaign to reform the safety net are becoming a distant memory. But never has innovative thinking on social policy been so necessary.

First, the net to catch the poor. It is unacceptable for society to abandon to desperation the victims of social and economic forces that are beyond their control. In former times, and in many developing countries today, such people were let loose into a parallel society of destitution, crime, or dependence on charity. The distinction in communist China between those who belong to "units" and therefore receive social security benefits – the iron rice bowl – and those on the outside with no access to those benefits, is exactly the same as the division between ins and outs – vagrants, beggars and desperadoes – in John Locke's England. Welfare measures should ideally reach all the needy, since, relatively speaking, society has enough wealth to take care of them. Of course, society does *not* succeed in reaching all of them. We still have our outs, those who slip beyond the periphery of even provincial and municipal welfare programmes, the homeless and ne'er-do-wells. In fact, experts tell us that polarization is increasing, that more and more people are becoming marginalized by rapid economic, social, and technological change.

Support for the needy – the unemployed, the unemployable, the destitute, the infirm, the old – should be the main focus of government in the social welfare area. "Welfare" in its narrower sense is equated with social assistance or income support. Although government is not very good at saving the economy or inventing jobs, it has a primary responsibility to assist those affected by economic and social change. Unemployment Insurance (UI) and the Child Support scheme administered by the federal government, and welfare programmes administered by provincial and municipal governments for others, including those who are not eligible for UI, are the main instruments in use. To all intents and purposes, the old age pension belongs to income support rather than income security, or soon will, since the clawback will eventually tax back most or all of it for those above the poverty line – a fact that calls in question the need for this instrument, but I will turn to that later.

Real problems, some of them identified already, have developed in this area. I read in recent media analysis of the Axworthy reforms that, besides the million Canadians who are unemployed, an additional three million are on some kind of welfare. Even if this figure is a million out, it is appalling. It means that close to 15 per cent of our population are being supported by those who work. This is a terrible indictment of the state of our economy and perhaps also of our society. The cost of this assistance is staggering. So are the social costs, the despair, the psychology of dependence, the lack of productivity. Although they are essential, services to the needy have to have a financial limit and should include means of tackling the social costs of dependency.

Of course, the means under discussion to address some of these problems are well known. I have no magic solutions beyond them. They include using welfare schemes as incentives to people to work and for training and education to make those who are employable better fitted for the job market. Rationalization and streamlining of assistance programmes cutting across federal-provincial lines, so that disparate programmes can be consolidated and "one-stop shopping" can be offered, would cut administrative costs. I have heard a federal official say that integrated management of federal schemes alone by "case managers" has saved thirteen dollars for every dollar invested in it. Some unitary system combined with incentives to move off income support programmes might pull all these programmes together and make them more economical – but there are big "ifs." All our experience with social engineering leads to scepticism about its promise. Few effective mechanisms tend to originate in the stodgy corridors of government. The non-governmental sector often devises much better means of fitting people for rapid changes in the work environment, especially in good times. Centuries-old social experimentation has been carried on by religious movements, which sometimes provide people with new focus and direction. These days there is much emphasis on secular forms of conversion, changing psychology, orienting people toward their problems in new ways so that they find their own means to resolve them.

A newspaper column on the Axworthy reforms said they were "Americanizing" Canada's welfare system, that they were right-wing and lacking in compassion, as if the old "He who does not work will not eat" rubric were being applied. Others have criticized hints of reductions in funding or at least the idea of establishing financial limits for welfare programmes. I do not believe these are germane. They most often come out of a tired and uncritical faith in the efficacy of government action. We need to bear in mind both sides of the issue, needs as well as resources.

First, there will always be people who cannot help themselves and who cannot survive without assistance – the disabled, the ill, and many of the aged. The cards are stacked too heavily against many others for self-support to be within their power, single parents, for example, some of the time. However, for many – the majority I suspect – there is no reason for dependence to be a permanent condition and there is nothing compassionate about cultivating it or creating semi-hereditary "proles." We do no justice to the children of welfare families by encouraging them to accept such a way of life as natural. No better seedbed could be invented for that other very costly form of "state support" not yet mentioned, the prison system.

Secondly, state funding is not unlimited. Even if the safety net is given priority, we can only do what we can afford. If Canada's fiscal nightmare becomes catastrophic, *no one* will receive income support. There will be no compassion in that. We are already in excess of reasonable limits for expenditure in this field, exemplified by the large deficits that built up during the last recession in welfare areas. These have been turned around by tightening up on qualifications for receiving benefits and even reducing payments. These are harsh measures but limits are inevitable. I apologize for the cliché, but there is no free lunch. Someone always pays. In the absence of national fiscal integrity there will be no one with the resources to pay.

The universal social security system, income security as opposed to income support, has become a fixture of modern life. Health insurance and retirement income security are the principal instruments. Health insurance has been a relative success. It is unfair, and it is unacceptable to the current generation of Canadians, to be in thrall to financial institutions, doctors or hospitals, because of accidental susceptibility to disease. This remains a common circumstance in the United States, where people must finance medical costs through costly private insurance or, worse still, massive loans. Indeed, state health insurance has been a factor in keeping down the costs of medical care in Canada and has demonstrably kept down the medical costs of households.

Despite these factors, there is serious trouble in our health system that must be diagnosed and treated. Like UI and welfare deficits, the increased cost load for health insurance agencies has become staggering and the integrity of the system has been called into question. It has led to efforts to trim coverage and reduce hospital services, and to the phenomenon of "extra billing." This kind of shotgun approach has the disadvantage of leaving people without certain benefits.

Of course, the cost of a health care system needs to be evaluated overall. We need to look at both private and public expenditure, at what "consumers" receive for their investment and at their personal cost. This would provide a basis for comparison among health care systems in different countries. But there is enough evidence to suggest that we need to reexamine our system, its strategic objectives as well as its delivery systems. We need to ask whether we spend too much as a society on health care and, if we do, how we can reduce costs without significant loss to our people. The recent comparisons the federal government has drawn with European expenditure, even if they ignore some differences in real costs and in the standard of care, are enough cause to study the issue afresh and not accept pat answers. Certainly there is waste. A psychology, an expectation, that disregards costs and seeks to maximize benefits has been created. The demand for services has constantly increased, to the point of exceeding the capacity of institutions and the medical profession to meet it. Some services appear to have deteriorated or have fallen short of demand. The waiting rooms of specialists are chock full and waiting time is agonizingly slow. Many people not on their deathbeds but requiring surgery face long, annoying, even painful and life-threatening delays. They often resort to the tried and true practice of pull: whom you know is more important than what disease you have. A doctor in the family or among one's close friends is a tremendous asset. Meanwhile, new treatments, drugs and technologies are mushrooming in number and in cost, many of them not affordable under current plans.

We have been living too high on the hog. A health insurance scheme has to be managed wisely. It needs to establish a basic standard of services all Canadians have rightful access to, but it must also establish limits. No society has unlimited resources. There must be items left uncovered until funds can be found for them. Some have experience with private group plans that keep increasing levels of support without a premium increase. How? Through efficient management, introducing new services when the funds are available to support them, while remaining highly client-oriented. Provincial agencies seem to be trying to make adjustments, fitfully, but a public consensus is lacking. As a public, we demand too much. Media crusades deal with anomalies and special cases of need. We all applaud decisions to provide costly services to someone afflicted with a rare disease. How could anyone be so inhuman as to oppose them? But we have to change the psychology that ignores the costs of things and pushes us beyond the affordable level of service.

I mentioned that universal plans have already faced a number of adjustments, in particular the conversion of the Family Allowance programme and pensions to income support programmes. The surviving part of the universal social security system, the Canada Pension Plan and its Quebec equivalent, are problematic. I will discuss this state retirement income plan in the next chapter.

Governments, as long as they exist, will always be called on to perform certain services: licensing, passports, citizenship, traffic control, garbage collection. These are jobs that either should not or could not be done privately – you cannot have private issuance of passports or money. Even if the private sector could do garbage collection more efficiently than municipal governments, we could not leave it to the private sector to take action because garbage must be collected in the interest of good order and public health whether it is profitable to do it or not. Public institutions should manage or perform services where a significant benefit may result. Some rules of thumb for this area are that:

- there should be as few as possible of these;
- they should be limited mostly to essential services;
- the onus is on the government to show that it can provide services better than the private sector because we know that in general it does not;
- government organizations performing such services need to prove themselves capable of radically improved efficiency and service to the public;
- there are many existing areas that need a fresh look with a view to offloading them.

Now let us move on to means of paring back this plethora of functions to those that are essential and affordable, and to look at innovative, economical ways of doing the businesses we will still want government to perform.

CHAPTER FIVE

Out of Business

What businesses should government get out of partially or completely? Or, to put it more aptly for this stage of the discussion, what businesses are unaffordable? I would like to look at three areas, two of which I have already introduced

1. intervention in the economy and other spheres of national life;
2. parts of the social security area;
3. education.

The last of these, since it is a special subject that requires treatment at length, will be discussed in a chapter of its own. Another area that may need some study is foreign aid, but this is too complex a subject and involves too much specialized knowledge of foreign affairs to undertake here. I will make a few passing references.

There is not much new in this chapter, not much that plenty of consultants, experts, and officials have not thought of. A fairly comprehensive concept for offloading businesses of government exists at the federal level. The Massé Programme Review calls for justification of the role of government, especially the federal government, in all programmes. Still, there has been relatively limited and unfocused discussion of these matters in the public domain. Moreover, government itself has a long history of falling short of its own rational objectives. Although one hears that departments took the Massé review seriously, it would still surprise me a great deal if they took as hard and objective a look at the need for a governmental role in their programmes as an outsider would. Moreover, governments get frightened by the difficulties of transition. The very thought of the pain involved can turn off reformers before they even begin. Despite all the talk, it is far from clear that the will exists to make the major changes that are critically needed, and even less clear that ministers and public servants have been fully and permanently converted to the basic principles embodied in the reform. Equally, there is not yet a consensus in the community at large to support these changes. The polity to which you and I belong is inconsistent: we want more money in our pockets and smaller government but we squawk whenever we are affected by a government cutback.

I will try to adhere to what may be called the principle of the blank sheet. That is, I will look at objectives for reform or improved efficiency as if there were no need for transition, and government programmes were being created *ex nihilo.* I take this tack not because I discount the difficulties of transition, and still less because I see any virtue in impracticality, but to bring to bear a longer-term view on the issues. We need to think strategically, not simply day to day and month to month. If our vision of where we want to end up is a powerful one, if our objectives are clear and desirable, the pain of short-term change provides a weak argument against action.

The previous chapter has already pointed a finger at businesses of government that are candidates for abandonment: most of the costly, confused, and intrusive interventions government makes in our social and economic life. I would like to try to establish clearer guidelines for what should and should not be a governmental responsibility.

Aside from establishing the groundrules for the economy and providing regulatory mechanisms where the market cannot serve the public interest, efforts to manipulate the market should on the whole be abandoned. This includes subsidization, marketing boards, and all but a few of the remaining Crown corporations. To these I would add misusage of the taxation system.

Intervention in the market does not work. No organization in society, including government, possesses the qualifications to bring about economic prosperity and advancement better than the competitive market on its own. What we have learned from generations of experience is that intervention usually leads to economic distortions that result in prolonged government support and leave the taxpayer or the consumer footing the bill. At the same time, it interferes with natural processes of competition and adjustment that will set matters right eventually. Central direction also puts in place a bureaucracy that acquires too much power, wastes too many resources, and rarely knows when it has ceased to be relevant.

There are legitimate concerns about the effect that massive change has on people, but these should be addressed through the social safety net and be focused on individuals. I do not doubt that a troubled industry is a social, not an individual, issue. Workers who are displaced deserve all possible assistance, but trying to address such problems by freezing or distorting sectors of the economy is terribly costly, does not work (at least not for very long), and interferes with processes of adjustment that may in time bring greater benefit. Imagine where we would be if newspapers and governments had given in to the unions on the issue of offset printing three decades ago, or if we still had "firemen" on diesel locomotives? Some jobs would have been saved, at least for a while, but these industries would have been paralyzed, their development arrested, their capacity to compete undermined. Technological change is now happening so rapidly that the workforce of the future will need to be much more flexible than at present in adapting their skills or acquiring new ones.

Subsidies, grants to small business, funding for regional development, and similar transfers are also fatally flawed, whether used as seed money to foster a particular industry or as dole money to keep an uneconomic enterprise afloat for "national interest" reasons. Those who provide such grants and contributions are not subject to the discipline of the market; they do not have to succeed and make money, as a bank does. Moreover, subsidies lead to abuse by the private sector. What company will not fatten its revenues by taking a hand-out? A national interest case can always be invented to justify such assistance. Do you want these widgets produced in Cleveland or Atlanta rather than in Oshawa or Cambridge? Then, give me the dough. Once in existence, a subsidy is treated as an entitlement and it becomes permanent. Special interest lobbies are usually effective in preventing their abolition. When a grant is used to keep an enterprise afloat, its continuation becomes even more crucial. Yet, I would be very surprised if any but a small percentage of these measures is successful. A transition step might be to operate such programmes as bankers do, treating grants as loans, then let them slide out of government's hands into the private sector, to live or die as the market determines.

Subsidy schemes were very much alive in Bob Rae's Ontario. Grants to the car industry and to bus manufacturers, the latter on the familiar grounds that a high-tech, quality-product industry might go under, and significant employment be lost unless it receives support, are cases in point. One must look at their long-term impact. Do these policies create the conditions for long-term sustainability, including for secure employment in a viable industry? What is the impact of their costs to the taxpayer? What they have done is deepen the provincial deficit and lower Ontario's credit rating, which are consequences that negate any short-term gains. And once in, governments cannot easily get out. By the time they do, the costs will have greatly outweighed the benefits.

In the last chapter I mentioned federal subsidies to education. Some of the arguments that question subsidies to industry apply here. The federal government is no better at assessing longer-term needs in, say, basic research in the universities than it is in discerning shorter term R and D priorities in the business community. Moreover, it provides assistance to universities through too many channels, with no strategic coordination. Even foreign aid is playing a role, all the more since taking on new non-economic fields of "development" (democratic development and human rights, for instance). Perhaps provincial governments can do little better, but they do have constitutional responsibility for education and most readily fulfill the public role someone must play in establishing education priorities. Academics and researchers themselves are all in favour of a multiplicity of instruments – all the better to increase their chances of obtaining funding. But from a strategic perspective, the field is a mess: too many instruments, too many objectives, no clear mandate.

History has more or less decided the issue of subsidies and market manipulation (e.g., marketing boards) for us. Governments are moving away from them. There is a broad consensus in society that they should do so, including in the business community. International trade law resulting from GATT's Uruguay Round is obligating governments to phase out such measures. Canada, one of the world's most active and intrusive managers of the agricultural sector, will be undergoing difficult adjustments but they are long overdue. Marketing boards discriminated against consumers by making products more costly for them and acted as a non-tariff barrier against foreign suppliers. How easy and tempting it was to rally 'round the flag to defend such bodies! Now parties to the GATT have to replace such measures with tariffs, and then gradually phase out the tariffs.

For political reasons, we will probably never be able to refrain from some regional development measures. If we have them we must manage them well, making use of whatever lessons have been learned from the past, but on the whole we should move away from them. Although a fraction of investment by government may legitimately catalyze business, efforts to stimulate economies artificially fail most of the time, while remaining a huge cost to the taxpayer. They may keep an industry alive, but they do nothing to create a basis for self-sustaining, competitive economic activity. Such assistance also readily declines into mere patronage. To what extent have such approaches to disseminating wealth reduced local incentive to develop economically viable industries? Are the economic backwaters of Canada any less backwaters as a result of "regional development" policies? The government role in regional development needs to be rethought from the ground up. The issue of addressing poverty, for example, ought to be treated in a social security context and assistance provided to affected individuals – but not necessarily to stay in place. Incentives are necessary to allow people to move to where the jobs are. A policy of maintaining people in place, even though the economy of a region may be unable to support them, is economically unwise. Depressed regions might be able to make more of a go of it if they were able to make a fresh start, focusing on newer, more promising sectors.

Governments manage many things, not only economic enterprises. They run schools, hospitals, airports, waterway systems, and seaports. They provide postal services. They manage public works projects, construction of buildings, roads, and other facilities. They run utilities and local transportation companies. They are owners and managers of national enterprises, railways, airlines, nuclear power, and communications companies. During the Trudeau years, a "Just Society" panache (influenced by Johnson's "Great Society" no doubt) overwhelmed politicians' perceptions of the limits of society's resources, government became the owner of last resort, when, for example, acting to keep small aircraft manufacturing companies alive. Government began to compete with private companies in fundamentally private parts of the economy like the petroleum industry.

With the privatization of Canadian National Railways now being pursued by the Liberals, all the main monuments of the era of the Crown corporation will have disappeared. This is a major achievement. Not so long ago, the Crown corporation was being used as an instrument to bail out uneconomic enterprises, especially in the aircraft industry. However, bailouts are unwise, not only because they are too costly for the public purse to bear, but because they are at odds with competitive market forces. In general, governments recognized that Crown corporations, even if more flexible and market-driven than government departments, are less effective than enterprises fully subject to competitive forces. Many have been money-losers. Moreover, governments find it difficult to compete in the market without using their immense power to dominate it. They have many tools to help tilt the board in favour of their own enterprises.

The case of the Canadian Broadcasting Corporation has always been viewed as special. Nevertheless, it has not been immune from repeated cutbacks, and questions about its relevance are now very much in the air. Is the CBC truly necessary from a public interest perspective? The answer is much less clear than it once was, however strongly one may feel about the CBC's historic role. Now that the air waves are overflowing with television channels and the "Death Star," satellite access to well over a hundred channels, threatens all national control, how much control can be maintained in practice? I suspect we have reached a point at which only egregious and unacceptable controls could block out the flood of signals that are about to overwhelm us. Alternatively, in an era of small "niche" broadcasters, are there other ways for the CBC to achieve its objectives, ways less costly to the taxpayer? CBC Radio, although its niche is small and elitist, has perhaps fulfilled a national objective at a reasonable cost. Its service – a unique formula nowadays in broadcasting – is a national asset that I confess I would be loath to lose. But what does CBC-TV contribute to national life? And how tough should government, through the CRTC, be in imposing "policy" on a sphere whose independence from governmental authority – like the freedom of the press – is so critical? And should governments seek to mould or obstruct the inclinations of consumers as they face the goodies of so vast a marketplace? As for myself, I resent any interference in my freedom to have access to media offerings of my choice and I am at a loss to know how I become less Canadian as a result of exercising it. We can hardly refuse to grant the principle of free choice simply on the grounds that some people have less sophisticated taste and judgment than others. In the current circumstances, they will find ways to exercise that choice anyway.

The above is not an argument for abolishing the CBC, but it does suggest that it be rethought and redesigned from the ground up, in light of cost, changing circumstances in telecommunications and the national interest, and not just trimmed around the edges as governments continue to do.

Direct government involvement survives in many areas, of course, and will do so for reasons set out in the last chapter, that is either for reasons of paramount national interest or because the government is the receptacle of last resort. Nevertheless, all cases need to be sifted through critically in order to rid ourselves of those that have outlived their usefulness and refit others, as radically as necessary, to serve the public better and at lower cost.

There are three common models that get government out of businesses it should not be in. There are others, and there are hybrids, but these three, at least, are plausible ones.

The first is outright privatization. The privatization schemes of the Mulroney Government in the 1980s were, in fact, an impressive start. They arose out of sources that at first did not seem promising to us: Reaganism in the United States and Thatcherism in the United Kingdom, that were soon aped all over the developed world by a suddenly neo-conservative age. However, by any criteria they were essential and they were effective. They proved that the monolith of big government could be broken up and the psychology of drift challenged. They unloaded burdens that would have magnified the cost of government during the recent recession to a potentially disastrous degree.

Why did privatization not achieve more than it did in digging us out of our financial mess? Of course, these were early days. There was limited acceptance of a major change in the role of government, and little sensitivity to the proportions our financial and economic crisis had already assumed. Enterprises were spun off slowly and amidst a great deal of controversy because they were seen as national symbols or national assets, Air Canada being an example. The Tories should not bear the brunt of the blame for this. The opposition parties and we, the public, had a substantial share in it. Another factor, for which they bear greater responsibility, was that in the years between the recessions the government did not take its own rhetoric about public indebtedness seriously enough. The Mulroney Government was a pork-barrel regime, intent on staying in power and on rewarding its supporters after their many years in the wilderness. Public enterprises, boards, commissions (not to mention the Public Service proper and even embassies overseas) were all pawns in the patronage game.

The positive outcome is that privatization is now an accepted means of unloading government services capable of standing on their own feet. Programme Review is giving rise to widespread privatization not only of Crown corporations but of many other government operations.

A second model is contracting out. A variant is what was once called "partnership," a joint venture with the private sector for delivery of a service. Contracting out is most useful where government should act as the arbiter of the public interest but a large part of the service can be delivered more effectively and cheaply by the private sector. Highway construction and maintenance is an example. Officially, the federal government has a policy, promulgated and controlled by the Treasury Board, of encouraging contracting with private businesses. Unfortunately, the achievements have been slim. The programme has moved so slowly that by May 1994, several years after it was promulgated, a Treasury Board official admitted at a seminar that only one major contract had been let. Private entrepreneurs have found themselves, as usual, entangled in red tape. Bureaucrats admit that this is the case and titter about the way of the world, or the two worlds of government and business, but companies either become discouraged or are forced to play ancient bureaucratic games.

Government has some concerns that are not entirely illegitimate: its traditional models for contracts require scrupulous fairness: putting out tenders and accepting them on the basis of price, quality, and the public interest. A "partnership" is a big undertaking financially and much longer term than the usual fiscal year-bound contract. Fears of getting stuck with a single private partner or service-provider do need to be addressed. There need to be safeguards to prevent private sector entities from acquiring the same protection from competition that has long plagued the Public Service, and there need to be service standards they are obligated to meet at pain of loss of the contract. But I fear it is the novelty of such ideas, bureaucratic inertia, and lack of commitment that have been the major causes of delay. The precedents for contracting, in public works and in ministries of transport, to take common examples, are cumbersome and control-ridden. Governmental organizations do not have the structure, the incentive or the risk-taking capacity to make more radical contracting practices work, though they certainly have the capacity to ensure their failure.

A few positive developments are, nevertheless, occurring. Even the socialist ex-government in Ontario had at least spoken of farming a highway construction and management project out to the private sector. Toll roads are rather painful to motorists, but the advantages may offset the concerns. Users of the road will pay. Costs to the government will be lower. Maintenance costs will be covered. Standards for maintenance and repair are presumably part of the contract and must be met by the private contractor. We are not out of the woods: we have yet to see the scheme implemented and the delays in moving forward with Highway 416 do not engender confidence. But a good idea has been discovered and should be tried.

In fact, contracting out is a mechanism that could be very widely applied. It might bring some life and better service to urban public transport. It is already the norm for garbage collection and many municipal infrastructure projects, although it could probably be implemented more efficiently and with much higher regard for customers. Garbage collection is an example I put forward with hesitation. All who have come home to find containers pitched – their tops mutilated or lost – and the residue of garbage left on drive or lawn would find a visit to Germany or Austria on garbage collection day instructive. There they will see a highly mechanized, efficient, clean service in which workers take pride and about which clients have no reason to complain. Since similar methods have spread to Britain, it appears that the German system is being adopted as standard in the European Union.

The third model, which applies most aptly to sectors and industries that need to be responsive to public policy, would withdraw government from active management of many or most activities to become instead the setter and enforcer of national or provincial standards. The activity itself is managed by a non-governmental or private enterprise. This approach is applicable to many service industries: hospital administration, airports, perhaps municipal bus service, water services or other utilities, and transport or communications enterprises to the extent that market forces and a competitive environment fall short of serving public need. I see no reason why it should not be applied to postal services, which already know competition in the courier sector. It may apply very effectively in education, as the next chapter will argue. We should not exempt broadcasting if essential national objectives may still be met.

In many areas, we have no excuse to be other than thoroughly pragmatic. There is really no room for artificial ideological obstacles. Consider the Pearson Airport issue. Terminal 3 was developed as a private sector initiative. If not a resounding success financially, it is, I believe, keeping its head above water while providing a better environment than the older terminals for travellers, and regardless of whether the federal government got paid full value for its concession, it is keeping losses off the federal books. When the Chrétien Government fulfilled its campaign promise to cancel the deal to privatize the two older terminals, it did so ostensibly because it smelled a rat. However, the aftermath suggested that the government's intentions were, at least in part, ideological or political: ideological in that the idea of having a "non-profit" private entity run Pearson was wafted as an alternative; short-term and political in that very radical and impressive ideas for transforming the government's role in transport facilities – ideas indistinguishable from privatization – subsequently came rolling out of Transport Canada and the federal budget anyway.

In fact, there is no reason why profit-making private sector management should be eliminated from consideration, provided that it is overall a cheaper, better alternative for Canadians. If it is, profit incentives for the managers are not an additional cost to the public but may result in a reduction of costs and better service to the public.

At the same time, I would not deny that offloading government businesses to non-profit organizations may well be a viable, or even a better, option in a number of circumstances, especially where the activity is not likely to be profitable or private gain might skew its purpose. The advantage of operating outside many governmental rules and regulations may be the achievement of sleeker, more efficient administration, a more highly motivated staff and more innovative management. The bottomline is results, effectiveness in serving the public. Perhaps the model of the non-profit "business" would be more useful in hospital administration than outright privatization.

If the approach of confining government's role to the application of standards is to work, the standards-setting authority needs to be slim, sleek, and low-cost itself. If the overall cost of public policy and private management is as great as or greater than the cost of government management, no gain will have been made. It must be a condition that the reduction in government administration lead to large savings. These must not be eaten up by putting a worse, less efficient, more unwieldy bureaucracy in place of the old operational one. People have spoken of the tendency in the U.K. for such authorities to fill the space vacated as a result of the Thatcher and Major public service reforms. When they do so, it is not on the basis of public need; it is bureaucratic expansionism once again at work.

Some may see in these concepts a turning of the pages of history back to bygone days when most things were privately run and the public interest manifestly not served. Public utilities and many transportation companies gradually came under public management and ownership because they were ill-coordinated, had serious shortcomings in providing public service, and in the end were uneconomical. Would municipal transit commissions, which all have big deficits and are subsidized by the public purse, fly as private companies today? Would they ensure that the old and the infirm have access to appropriate services?

I would like to make four points. First, let us not underestimate the extent to which public interest was served by the private sector. The massive subway system of London, the largest city in the Victorian world, was essentially developed through private investment and managed privately for a time. Londoners still live with the oddities of a public transport system that was developed higgledy-piggledy, not in a planned manner, yet, granting this, its age and the size of the city it serves, is it not one of the most serviceable in the world? Secondly, the rules of the game have substantially changed. Governments are now much more adept than they were one hundred years ago at ensuring compliance with standards and an adequate level of service by non-governmental institutions to the public. Thirdly, parts of such enterprises may be profitable and other parts not. If governmental spending can be narrowed to the areas that need support, airports in the north for example, privatization of the rest might save money overall. Fourthly, when privatization is economically unfeasible but the activity remains essential, the case for private sector management disappears and favour shifts back to the public sector.

As the last chapter suggests, help for the needy is an essential role of government. Nevertheless, it must be affordable. Affordability may be attained by establishing expenditure limits, by streamlining administration, and by streamlining the system itself, for example, by combining delivery mechanisms. UI should be kept separate, in my view, but run as a self-supporting insurance business. When originally conceived, that is what it was: an insurance business. Somewhere along the way, the insurance element became a sham and UI turned into an income support scheme, whose substantial deficits were covered by federal government revenue. Tightening up on rules to save money, as the government has done in the past year, is all very well but what is really needed is a more radical clean-up, in effect returning UI to what it was at its inception.

Whether the Child Support scheme, successor to Family Allowances, and the old age pension, now that it is exiting the universal social security area, need to have an identity distinct from other forms of social assistance, like provincial welfare, is doubtful. A single delivery mechanism would cut red tape, ensure against duplication and fraud, and decrease the cost to taxpayers. It would need, at least administratively, to cut across the federal-provincial divide. A current idea is to attack this through administrative rather than constitutional means. One thought would be to have national standards, as in medicare, joint federal-provincial funding, and provincial administration of this assistance. Additional reforms would need to be built in to a redesigned system, such as incentives to promote a return to the work force and to accept retraining. These would help to break down the psychology of dependence among the employable poor.

An idea more popular some years ago than now and supported at various times by figures on both the right and the left is the negative income tax or the guaranteed annual income. Studied during the Nixon Administration in the U.S., and by Marc Lalonde as Health and Welfare minister during the Trudeau years, it foresaw uniting all help for the needy in a single instrument implemented through the tax system. It would establish a minimum income standard to which all "taxpayers" with less than the standard would automatically be raised. They would receive a sort of "refund" of taxes they have not paid. Leftists liked the concept because it would ostensibly wipe out poverty at one blow. Conservatives and classical liberals – Milton Friedman is an example of the latter – liked the idea of simplified administration and the freedom of choice the poor would have to spend their income in the free market as they wished (rather than having to spend food stamps on food, and so on, which restricted their freedom).

No government has proceeded with the guaranteed annual income and it is probably as well that they did not. Most often, they shied away because of its costs. We can understand that argument better than the politicians and theorists of the 1970s who considered the notion; more costly social programmes would have mired us even more deeply in indebtedness than we are now. A second problem is that guaranteed income would reduce the incentive to work and increase dependency on the state to a greater extent even than current programmes. Why work if you can make a decent living by doing nothing? We do not need to expand the phenomenon of dependency; it is socially and economically harmful. Today's thinking, as exemplified in McKenna's New Brunswick, is moving in the direction of welfare with built-in incentives to work. For reasons already spelled out at some length, that is surely the right direction in which to go. A third problem is that a "negative income tax" would overload even further the taxation system and confuse its objectives. Inevitably, some rules other than mere income level would be required to determine eligibility and to ensure fair implementation, and – lo and behold! – Revenue Canada would be head and shoulders into the welfare business. Nevertheless, the guaranteed income concept does get one thing right: the simplification of welfare instruments.

The universal social security system requires somewhat more detailed treatment. The stuffing has already been taken out of the universality of the system and the electorate has got used to its decreasing role. It is time to remodel much of the rest of the system.

The ideology of universality, as it used to exist, may be expressed in three basic tenets:

1. welfare programmes must be universal, but in addition;
2. governments must implement them;
3. governments can implement them most cheaply and in the best public interest.

The first means that certain benefits deemed universal need to be meted out to everyone, not just the needy. Although widely shared, this may be termed a socialist dogma in that it is a drum the CCF/NDP have tended to beat most loudly in Canada. The great reformers of a former day, Stanley Knowles, Tommy Douglas and others, looked back at older welfare systems based on a "means test" that accorded aid only to those who could prove they needed it. Shades of the Poor Law, welfare officials were intrusive and nasty and the poor were made to go through hoops of humiliation to qualify for assistance. Almost all political parties have since stood solidly behind universality. The result was a rational, businesslike, non-discriminatory universal welfare system but one that has proved enormously costly and at times produced glaring anomalies: millionaires receiving seven dollars a month Family Allowance payments or fifty dollar old age pension cheques. Intrusiveness has, on the whole, been overcome by using the tax system to determine income level. This does seem to me a fair use of taxation data as long as it does not require the tax system to have or to keep all its other misguided social welfare functions. There also needs to be a condition that such data may be used for other than taxation purposes only with the taxpayer's consent, since it is personal information.

The dogmas that government should implement these programmes and that it can do so most cheaply are closely interconnected. They rest on the principles that the private sector, being out for itself, cannot be counted on to provide a fair, cheap service to people, that inequities would result (because the rich would be able to pay higher premiums and obtain better coverage) and that universal schemes increase the financial base and correspondingly decrease costs, much as a group insurance scheme is less costly than a personal insurance plan. We heard the last argument again recently when ex-premier Rae flirted with the concept of public automobile insurance.

In the current environment, we need to move beyond these positions. We know, for instance, that government agencies tend to be less efficient than the private sector, so the overhead in government tends to be higher. They do not face the same discipline of the bottomline or the rigours of competition that private sector businesses face. Many parts of the private sector, moreover, are now more socially responsible, a consequence of shrewder consumers and better service orientation in the business community. Social responsibility has become part of the curriculum in business schools. However, we should not base a judgment on a belief that people are better than they are or on blind faith in the private sector. If the private sector is more responsible, this is largely because it makes sense in the long-term. Government retains a responsibility to monitor business practices and ensure that public standards are met and the public interest is served.

The third dogma, based on the idea of a universal captive clientele, may be sound enough on actuarial principles – I would not presume to judge. On the other hand, it is a handy ideology to defend monopoly, and monopolies are not known for their efficiency, cost-effectiveness or quality of customer service. A private sector monopoly might be more efficient than a public sector one, but it would need to be carefully regulated – as in the Bell Canada model – whereas competition is likely to be a better means of minimizing cost and maximizing the value of service. Which system is the most economical and best serves the public should be settled by testing them, not merely debating their philosophical merits.

As a result of gradual shifts in policy during the Mulroney years, the public has come to accept a paring back of the universal welfare system. Universal child support and income support for the aged are wasteful in cases where families and individuals do not need them. At present, only medicare and the national pension plan (including the Quebec Pension Plan) survive.

What about health insurance? Provincial health insurance schemes have so far been relatively successful but, as noted, they are in increasing financial difficulty. Perhaps we should not tinker too much with programmes that are on the whole effective. Could private insurance companies, even under tough government guidance, do better than medicare has done? We see across our southern border a system of health insurance that is wholly private (except for medicare for the elderly). It leaves tremendous power in the hands of private insurance companies. Premiums, I believe, are generally high, higher than public health insurance in Canada, coverage less complete and costs to the consumer, by all reports, greater. There is competition, some streamlining to provide better, quicker service and more choice for the consumer, and companies do have to operate as businesses or go out of business. But the evidence suggests that we get more service at less cost in Canada. Thus, trimming, conservative management and improved efficiency may be enough – may avoid throwing the baby out with the bath water.

On the other hand, higher efficiency might be obtained by increasing the distance between the delivery mechanisms for health insurance and the governments that set the rules. The option of reducing governments' role to one of setting standards and contracting operations to a non-profit or private sector entity should be considered seriously if it could maintain levels of service and reduce costs. A non-profit agency is likely to be more attractive to Canadians. The standards would, at a minimum, equate to those now set by the federal government for provincial programmes, ensuring universality, portability, and affordability (eliminating extra billing, as now). Closest to the current practice would be for governments to fund the delivery agency or agencies (profit or non-profit) through taxes or premiums paid to government. At least two other models exist or have been extensively studied. In one, the premiums would be paid to the administering agency or agencies – which could be a number of private insurers. The options for a health care system that were under consideration in pre-Newt Gingrich Washington would be a version of this model. The Hilary Clinton proposal was for essentially private insurance systems, but ones subject to government regulation or standards to ensure universality. This fairly modest departure from a wholly private health care system still failed to find significant support in Congress and is now dead.

In another model, funding would be mixed. The supplementary Public Service Health Plan and the Public Service Dental Plan, group insurance schemes for federal employees, may serve as examples of this in that there tends to be a mix of premiums and employer funding, while the insurers are exclusively private companies. I doubt that our society wants so radical a change. However, options like these need to be explored and assessed much more assiduously than I suspect is occurring if we are to be serious about understanding the prospects for improving cost-effectiveness. The greatest weakness of the current model is that it is treated as unquestionable. Dogmas end up by leading us astray. Perhaps the funding difficulties in health insurance are a sign that the system has gone astray in significant respects. We need to keep our minds open and study the alternatives. In any case, medical insurance does need to be run more as a business, more at arm's length from the policy-makers, more self-sustaining in terms of its funding, whatever mechanism is selected.

The area of pensions, including the Canada Pension Plan (CPP) and its Quebec equivalent, seems to me unambiguously one that government should abandon.[1] This is for several reasons. First, the scheme has been mismanaged. A devastating series of articles in the *Globe and Mail* by Andrew Coyne in mid-August 1994, suggested that for the first time benefits paid were higher than revenues, both contributions and earnings, in 1993.[2] As our population ages, the funds can be kept out of the red only by dramatically raising contribution levels, something that has already begun but that is destined to become a much more terrible burden for our children. The QPP is slightly better off than the CPP, but not much. A number of factors have led to this situation but a key one is that the funds have not been run as businesses. For example, they have been used for cheap loans to governments, federal and provincial. They have been another cheap source of revenue for institutions that have never learned to live within their income.

As an aside, it is even more worrying to consider the appalling state of the Public Service Superannuation Plan, the registered pension plan for federal public servants. I understand that it has built up no fund at all. It uses employee contributions as revenue and pays pensions as if they were salaries. If our government ever reaches a point at which it is unable to match expenditure with its total intake from revenue and borrowing, the retirement income of hundreds of thousands of former wage-earners (including the writer) will be jeopardized.

Secondly, the value of the CPP to the pensioner is often not worth its cost. It was designed to provide retirement income to those salary earners who do not have the benefit of a registered pension plan large enough to support them in retirement. However, the pension income it provides is really very little (a maximum of about $713 per month in 1995), hardly a retirement income, more like another of the bits-and-pieces social security payments of which our system has tended to consist. Contributions are based on income a wage-earner receives while working, but only up to a maximum of (currently) $34,900 – an average Canadian wage. The retirement benefit, though based on contributions (thus, this does not appear to be a disguised income equalization programme), hardly makes a significant difference to middle and higher income people. Why should they be a part of the system? Why should anyone who wishes to not take another approach? Why should the system be universal? The CPP seems to produce another of those anomalies we often find in universal systems, where middle and higher income people are concerned (like the millionaires who, as mentioned, received $7 per month in Family Allowance payments in about 1950). They can do without the CPP and so could many others.

Do those who pay into the CPP get full value for their money, as they unquestionably do from many registered pension plans?[3] They may – if they live long enough – but there is no certainty that they will. Compare the CPP to a normal retirement investment plan. If a conservative investor puts aside $20,000 over his working years (the contribution of a low to average wage-earner), he would, with interest or capital gains, have at least three times that amount by the time he retires. He would need to receive CPP payments of about $600 per month for eleven to twelve years to match what he would have from a private fund. CPP contributions have practically no cash value for the contributor.[4] Their value resides solely in the income paid out by the government. Given a choice, prudent and farsighted people would usually opt to manage this money as part of a larger retirement plan of their own.

One other point of interest for beneficiaries of many registered pension plans is that CPP benefits are cut back drastically at age 65. The benefit is only about 40 per cent of the norm in this instance. The ostensible reason for this is that the plan compensates for the reduction. I must say, however, that the rationale is agonizingly elusive. Looking at the CPP alone, a person subject to such a reduced pension will virtually never receive value for money from the plan.

The CPP was probably misconceived from the start and should be phased out now (on the understanding that there would be transition measures and those who have paid into it will receive a fair return). There is no reason why people should not be able to manage their own retirement funds, with the help of the plethora of reputable financial institutions and advisers that are around. The additional income the CPP programme is intended to provide could come from allowing a higher level of contributions to RRSPs, for example. Government may wish to establish some standards for such contributions, including a minimum contribution, a lock-in arrangement for this minimum amount and its earnings, standards of eligibility for financial institutions and types of investments, and additional deposit insurance or guarantee arrangements to protect pensioners against the failure of private institutions.[5] This degree of intrusiveness by government may cause a true liberal to blench, but it has a point. Wage-earners who do not put money away, those who invest unwisely, and those who are the victims of developments beyond their control might end up as charges to the state or burdens on society in their retirement years. Such burdens should be minimized. I am not sure this would be justifiable, however. There would be less interference in our private affairs if the government limited itself to providing incentives for retirement savings, as it does now for RRSPs, or got out of the field altogether and focused a part of the resources now going into the CPP on income assistance for the needy. In any event, beyond any minimum premium the government might establish, it would be the wage-earner who would be responsible for arranging for his retirement income through registered pension plans, contributions to RRSPs and other savings and investments.

Whatever safeguards there may need to be, the object should be to put greater responsibility on the shoulders of us wage-earners to manage our own futures. We must have greater freedom to do so and the maximum latitude to make our choices. The issue of retirement income is in large part a private one, after all, and the onus should be on the people, not on government, to decide which savings options they prefer.

CHAPTER SIX

EDUCATION

No challenge is likely to be more sensitive than one to public education. I am myself a beneficiary of the public education system and I have always been a firm believer in it. The integrity of public education is a peculiarly North American concept: it developed on this side of the Atlantic long before it was fully accepted in Europe. It brought the benefits of education to a far broader range of people than used to be the case anywhere else. It was more suited to democratic societies, subversive of class distinction. Egerton Ryerson in Ontario, and the founders of public school systems in the other provinces and the American states are legitimate heroes. The initiative of our American neighbours in this century to make higher education almost universal, a strategy Canada has taken up since the 1960s, is especially praiseworthy, even if standards of higher education have tended to be affected. Education departments remain the elite ministries of provincial governments. So clear is the bias in favour of public education that Quebec's late development of such a system during the Quiet Revolution of the 1960s was seen as, and truly was, one of the potent signs of its entry into the modern age.

Most Canadians would not dream of questioning the concept of public education. In our experience, the alternative tends to be a private school system that is expensive, as for the most part it caters to the privileged, and, even then, only in a few outstanding cases is of unquestioned quality. Alternatively, non-elite private schools are often of questionable academic merit, like some of the so-called visa schools catering to foreign student demand, or the cram schools for drop-outs from which some of them grew. Other "independent" schools raise concerns because they are sometimes of a religious character, or because they are controversially experimental. We fear reverting to a Charles Dickens world of sleazy entrepreneurs, mixed or inadequate standards, and huge class distinctions.

Nevertheless, the failings of the education system in Canada are so great and the costs so high that it is more obviously in need of radical reform than almost any other part of the public sector. I speak as an outsider and a "customer," not of course as a teacher, expert, or administrator. I have been through the Ontario public system myself, mostly in the 1950s, and I have children in a public high school in the 1990s. From this admittedly limited perspective, how can these two periods be contrasted, what are the flaws in the current system, what are their causes, and what can be done about them?

Much can be said against the Ontario system in which I was educated some forty years ago. Its curriculum was rigid and traditional. It allowed limited choice. We were spoon-fed set texts at an appallingly slow, methodical pace. The standards achieved were not very high. No one then would have dreamed of introducing calculus to the curriculum. The priority was put on memorization, knowing facts, not on analysis. There was a little, but not nearly enough, streaming, which usually did no more than pile additional languages on the course-load of brighter students. Intelligence or academic achievement could be gauged from whether you were French-Latin-German, merely French-Latin, French only or, horror of horrors, in the sub-basement that could not handle languages at all and remained utterly remote from the possibility of reaching university. These were olden days, when the figure for university entrance was said to be 5 to 10 per cent of the numbers who started high school, and many students still left school for academic or economic reasons after Grade 10. In the fairly new suburban high school I attended, the population was still growing (the school was closed in the 1980s because of radical demographic change); I recall that we started with some thirteen classes in Grade 9 and had five in Grade 13, an ostensible decline of about 60 per cent. There were no community colleges, only Ryerson in Toronto filling a role in non-university post-secondary education.

What is to be said for education in that bygone age? Three things. One is that the curriculum was demanding in terms of study. The volume to be covered was large even if the standards were not especially high. Extensive homework was levied and it was very hard to do well, or even pass, without several hours of nightly study. However misdirected much of this work was, it taught us work habits that could be applied to other levels of study or other fields of work. Inevitably, we did learn something.

The second thing is that our education had breadth. We had to emerge knowing a set number of things – no doubt too set – about our language and literature, the languages and literatures of others, all the main sciences and mathematics, and what then passed for world history, which was admittedly centred on the West. All that I ever formally learned about Canadian history and most of my limited – and largely visual – capacity in the French language I learned in high school. Whatever the limitations of our schools then, there was a core curriculum that defined clearly what one had to know before entering broader society.

The other thing to be said in favour of schooling in the 1950s concerns the quality and dedication of some of the teachers. I can only point to a handful who were outstanding, but they left their mark and they encouraged in me a desire for post-secondary education that was entirely the product of the school system, since I inherited no such tradition from my home or family (not that I was discouraged). Now, I have no doubt that there are as many good teachers in any era but, just as the public sector seemed to be distinguished by a particularly dedicated group of senior public servants at that time, the school system was marked by a particular, almost religious, dedication. The notion of a teachers' strike was unthinkable. At the university level, take the University of Toronto for instance, there were academics and teachers with extraordinary public spiritedness. This was the era, among senior historians, of Careless, McNaught, Creighton, and Craig. The deepest impression on my young intellect was made by Northrop Frye, not just because of his brilliance but because of this world renowned scholar and theorist's commitment to pedagogy, his skill at creating illumination in the minds of rather pedestrian twenty-year-olds in stuffy old classrooms.

What about today? Formal standards have risen in some areas. I have mentioned mathematics. Of archaic and unreconstructed cast, my mind does not grasp why students now graduate from high school knowing practically no Euclid, but, since I cannot understand almost any of the mathematics that is studied, I believe humility is my only appropriate posture. In addition, today's high school student is opened to a wider understanding of the world and of languages. Choice has been increased to a significant extent, for example, in the social sciences. Despite the "destreaming" introduced by the levelling Rae administration in Toronto, somewhat more attention is given to bright students. There is more emphasis on thinking and less on memorizing than forty years ago. There are more research projects and essays.

Yet, public education is in shambles. A broad consensus considers that standards have collapsed and the quality of education is in disrepair. Much is written about getting back to the three Rs and there are spasmodic attempts to do so that never seem to succeed. Perhaps the current one in Ontario will. Its initiation is, at any rate, a sign that the provincial government has at last accepted the proposition that there is a quality problem.

Choice has been expanded to the point where the core curriculum has been emasculated and there is little depth of study. My children will leave high school knowing almost nothing about the history of their country; the thesis of the unwashed that Canadian history is "boring" has apparently been adopted by the schools. Whence cometh the next generation of civic consciousness if not from our schools? First language skills are deplorable. When my son took a writing course in Grade 10 (a good course, by the way), the teacher found knowledge of basic grammar, which is barely taught, so low that he handed out a composition textbook for additional study. It was *Learning to Write*, the same textbook I had used in 1960. It was not a bad book – I still bear the marks of its attempt to obliterate "major errors" – but has there been so little emphasis on English grammar since that time that no successor, no reworker of ways to instil in people pride in correctness of language, has challenged it in the field? And is it not appalling that proper grammar is not a mandatory part of the curriculum?

Worse still, not much knowledge is required to pass a course. It could be that grade inflation only means that numbers have been moved around, not that school is easier now, but I fear the worst. My children do tolerably well at what is considered our city's best public high school, but with barely an hour of homework on an average night and often none at all. They say, and since their grades do not suffer I have no reason to disbelieve, that they are completing all their assignments. Examinations, as we all know, are a bitter experience in general, so stress has been lifted by essentially eliminating all but one set. Poorer performers still have to write a second set in June but how many are they? My generation always wrote two sets of examinations apart from the optional finals. Grade 13 imposed, in addition, exceedingly tough mandatory final examinations, at least nine of them if you were graduating in one year, that were set and marked centrally under the direct auspices of the Department of Education. I wish there were a realistic way to test what people have learned without resorting to examinations; I know how poor they are as a touchstone for knowledge and the ability to think. The argument can be made that a better balance has been instituted by putting emphasis on work throughout the year. But by abandoning most examinations without putting an alternative and at least as sound system of measuring achievement in their place, our system has lost a major portion of its credibility.

When competitiveness was the rage in economic policy a few years ago, the federal government correctly fingered education as an area critical to productivity and our success as a trading nation. The decline in standards has terrible consequences for the economic well-being of our children and grandchildren.

We should remember that most school systems in the world today are more like mine from the 1950s than they are like contemporary North American education. Schools in Europe and in Asia, most particularly in the high-performance economies of Japan and Korea, are disciplined and oriented toward rote learning. Many of them have higher standards than my schools did – you have more advanced knowledge by the time you graduate – but the discipline of work has been the outstanding mark of both.

Significantly, people educated in such systems are now leading the economic revolution in Japan and the Pacific Rim. I do not attribute their economic success to this system alone – indeed, though it continues to produce very high standards of literacy, it is clearly not having the same economic results in the United Kingdom, or even on the European continent, as it is in Japan – but it does provide knowledge, habits of hard work, and a base or structure that supports continuing education during adult years.

The intriguing thing about Japan is that its university education is of poor quality; the raw material its industries have to work with is on the whole shaped at middle and high school levels. Little of this is highly technical in content, so that the Japanese model contradicts the view that we will do better if we focus education on vocations and applied science – make it "relevant." The additional ingredient in Japan has been the emphasis by companies on lifelong education, dubbed "continuous learning" in the management theory literature that focuses on increasing the quality of products and services. The wisdom of the Japanese approach is based on a revolution in the nature of knowledge and the way it is applied. Knowledge is growing and changing at so rapid a rate that no schooling, not even university education, can teach people all they will need to know throughout their careers. Employers therefore need to become educators, and they have done so in Japan. To return to the main point, a rather traditional, disciplined curriculum at public education levels appears to provide a better basis for "continuous learning" than our lax dilettantism. At the same time, no one would aver that such systems cannot be improved on. Imagine the product of a system that combined creativity with application and industry!

I can only express my great personal dissatisfaction and disappointment with the system as a parent – as a consumer – and hazard some personal observations concerning the reasons why we have such poor standards.

First, educational policy has become very confused, too driven by the flavour of the month in educational and psychological theory. A sort of wrong-headed "liberalism" – I hate to recall that terrible phrase, "the permissive society" – has prescribed as a primary objective the easing of the burden on the young, leading to the lifting of too many formal requirements. Perhaps under the guise of training children to become "whole" adults, education authorities, and the anti-intellectual parents who too often support them, have lost sight of how difficult learning really is: wisdom *does* have to be born out of midnight oil. The curriculum has become too diffuse. The wealth of options makes it possible to avoid being trained in Canadian "civics" and avoid learning other things a young adult ought to know. It is as though educators have not been sure what standards there should be. They move this way and that.

With indecision, moreover, there seems to have been a loss of energy or will to impose standards of excellence. Through a curious inversion, minimum standards have become maximum standards, a phenomenon that gives me great hesitation in embracing the latest effort at reform in Ontario, however needed it may be. The standards set at the ministry level, which are surely the minimum a student must meet in order to advance or graduate, are used as "benchmarks" – they are really the parodies of benchmarks – to elbow out higher standards of achievement. A better example, the International Baccalaureate, appears below but an amusing one is the "arts credit" required for the Grade 12 diploma. The Ministry of Education and many schools balk at accepting Royal Conservatory of Music certificates as substitutes for courses on the standard high school curriculum that are distinctly inferior in quality.

Why has this occurred? Ignorance? Chauvinism? Red tape? Egalitarianism? Rigidity? Arrogance? Most of these terms apply but let me add one: power. We have, in effect, a school system whose central authorities are both its standards-setters and its managers. And they can do anything they want.

Grade 13 examinations, when they existed, were harrowing, to be sure. Moreover, marking them centrally was costly, and given the size of the graduating population now, it would be all but impossible, but its elimination sacrificed a common, objective standard that nothing has replaced. OAC examinations are now set and marked by the schools in Ontario and the marks assigned, exceedingly inflated to my ancient brain, have lost all credibility. Now universities have to go by less rigorous rules of thumb, such as the university performance of graduates of particular schools, or "objective" placement tests. An examination system set centrally with at least "sampling" of local practice in marking would surely be possible and economical. The Bob Rae reforms did have in mind steps like these toward a strengthening of central control over the examination process.

Rocked by rapid technological change, our authorities have become concerned with "relevance" and preparation of people for the workplace. As a result, we do not give our young even a basic dose of what they ought to know. Like our southern neighbours, we suffer in comparison with Europeans and Asians from a lack of cultural tradition, a national character that might define for us clearer objectives for the educational process. The borrowed classical education of a former age once filled this role. It is no longer viable, if it ever was, but it did constitute an exacting standard for the educated person and we have nothing to fill the void. Flailing about as we have for more than a generation, we seem to have lost any concept of intellect or what is needed to train it. I do not wish to take sides in the humanistversus-professional debate about the purposes of education except to suggest that debate is misconceived: the bedrock of knowledge, useful or otherwise, is a trained mind, a mind that can think and express itself clearly, correctly and cogently. That is one reason why traditional forms of public education continue to prove their social worth in other societies.

Secondly, educational organizations, like public organizations in general, are self-serving and inefficient. They are, indeed, prime examples of the law of serving number one. In Ontario good-news blather has perpetrated the monstrous lie that we have the best public education system in the world. We have achieved a smugness unjustified by our standards, by the graduates we are producing, by comparative analysis or by our capacity to change and improve our system.

Let me take two examples. The first is the persistence of Grade 13, the Ontario Academic Credit year. Grade 13 has always been held up as the shining light of Canadian education, setting standards equivalent to the end of the freshman year in American universities and comparing itself with the "A-level" in Britain. The case has always been flawed. The fact is that people would learn much more in a university environment than in a high school. Grade 13 standards, traditional or contemporary, are not a patch on the A-levels, which involve vast reading and research and very tough examinations, quite beyond the ken of our schools. The dilution of the curriculum now means that most students could easily finish high school in four years, saving an important year of their lives and saving us taxpayers a bundle. A large number already reach the OAC year with several credits under their belt, though usually marginal ones in terms of their subsequent education. Why has a fifth high school year been preserved? Almost entirely to keep teachers employed. The system has lost all objectivity in judging this issue. Its standpoint is almost totally dictated by its own, not its clients', interests. The latest reform may finally do Grade 13 in, but the time it has taken to reach this crunch merely proves the inflexibility, foot-dragging, and regressiveness of our system.

Indeed, so incapable has our system become of providing a real academic challenge at the OAC level that many students are able to reduce their load to half-time, or to a half year. Full-time students are still supposed to enrol for six courses. I applaud this because it means that, if students have to be there at all, they will at least learn a little more. But what is the reason given by local high schools? They receive a larger provincial grant if they show a high number of courses being taken. Some students enrol for six and then drop at least one once the coast is clear.

In no other instance could the axe be so justifiably employed. The objective, abolition of Grade 13, is clear. The means, certain adjustments to the curriculum, are a mere matter of design and implementation. A reduction in teaching staff can be accomplished through attrition without imposing hardship or affronting dignity. Of course, for one year or a few the universities will have a much higher intake. This is becoming increasingly feasible as demographics weigh in and the number of young people of university age declines. Delay is mere procrastination.

Another sign of smugness in our system is its lack of awareness of quality elsewhere. It works in a fog, even at the university level. Consider the example of the International Baccalaureate, the IB. Most readers, not through their own fault, will not know what this is. It is a standard developed largely in the context of international schools, to allow peripatetic teens to meet the university entrance standards of their home countries. The French *lycée* system is comparable in setting an international standard for entry to French universities. The IB is demanding and sets a high standard. Where it is in use, it is limited to the better students, those most likely to go on to university. It involves two years of both intensive and extensive study (there are, for example, long, challenging reading lists), cultivates independence and creativity, requires good work habits and prescribes stiff examinations – but normally just one set, at the end of the two-year programme.

The IB is recognized by many European universities and increasingly in the United States. Who has heard of it in Canada? I read in a newspaper some time ago that Saskatchewan has introduced the IB for a quota of its better students, being limited by slightly higher tuition costs from expanding it further. To my knowledge, no other public system in Canada is using the IB. A recent syndicated newspaper report stated that Upper Canada College, an elite private high school in Toronto which has relatively high academic standards, had become so appalled by low standards and grade inflation that it was adopting the IB as its standard. Some other private schools offer the programme. In Ontario, ignorant administrators look down on such "foreign" standards, unable to imagine anything better than the Ontario system.

I am reminded of a story I once heard – it is about twenty years old. A young man from another province who had been educated at an elite American prep school and had already been accepted at Harvard and Yale sought admission to an Ontario university. Some younger and/or American staff members asked how the university could possibly refuse him when he had been accepted by such institutions. One old salt, only half in reply, mused, "What I don't understand is why his parents didn't send him to a public high school in Ontario." We continue to hear stories of this kind today and we continue to hear of arrogance in government. In a symposium in the *Ottawa Citizen*, Ottawa Board of Education Trustee Jane Dobell writes, "The Ottawa Board has been discouraged by provincial regulations from offering a Montessori alternative and the International Baccalaureate."[1]

Thirdly, we have become dominated by a misconceived form of egalitarianism. I made a snide indirect reference above to destreaming, a project of the former Rae Government to eliminate streaming into more and less advanced levels at the Grade 9 level. However, as I have noted, the lowest common denominator has actually dictated education in the province for a very long time, certainly since the Second World War, probably forever. The arguments put forward are largely social in nature: those who have greater difficulty learning will be disabused of the feeling that they are failures or "second-class citizens" if they are united with their peers of all levels of intelligence; they will actually learn better in the more stimulating atmosphere; the bright students will not suffer because teachers will be trained to cater to their needs.

I have no taste for this debate. For the sake of argument, I would concede the first two of these propositions but not the third. I object, rather, because such arguments turn the purpose of education upside down, making learning subservient to being well adjusted, and even then focusing on the social adjustment of the less gifted to the detriment of the well-being of faster learners. I have no quarrel with the fact that the adolescent years are critical: teenagers should without doubt emerge from high school with the best possible sense of their own worth and the respect of their peers. I believe, too, that "gifted" programmes of a particularly elitist kind may give smarter kids a false impression of their worth and their difference from others. (As a young man, I once participated as a teacher in an experimental summer school that attempted aggressively and explicitly to instil exactly such elitism in a largish group of bright young people. I had and continue to have the gravest doubts about it, especially because of the illusions of brilliance and superhumanity it was inculcating in some fine and intelligent, but hardly prodigious, young people.)

But the fact is, we cannot afford to neglect the best among us. Too much depends on them, for all of us. Their social and economic contribution will be greater than the contributions of others. We must recognize this. We cannot ignore it because it might hurt people's feelings. The purpose of education is not to make people feel good. We have to give them the best and get the best out of them. Moreover, self-esteem built upon a foundation of sand will soon crumble. There are good-news organizations (like most agencies of government) and even good-news countries (like historical Austria-Hungary, China under Mao, and with a vengeance, North Korea) in which fictional report cards, a mandatory positive self-image, and suppression of uncomfortable facts replace serious, constructive evaluation. For them as for individuals, the inevitable consequence, sooner or later, is breakdown: organizational, social, or personal. And, finally, the pre-eminent goal we ought to have is to encourage people to develop their own talents, abilities, and interests to the widest possible degree for their own sake. This has always been the heart of morality and is not less so today.

Just as material egalitarianism is wrongly conceived, so is educational egalitarianism. The object of public policy must be equality of opportunity, not any absolute equality of level. We cannot change the hard, perhaps "unfair" reality of the inequality of the genetic resources with which we are born. We must not blame anyone for nature's acts, but in turn, we must reward people for achievement.

A recent report found Canada to be second to Finland among industrialized countries in the proportion of GDP – 7.1 per cent – that is spent on education. The average is 6.1 per cent, and interestingly, the three lowest in the list, at about 5 per cent, the Netherlands, Germany, and Japan, count among the most productive economies in the world.[2] Given the decline in education and our relatively poor competitive position economically speaking, what has this huge investment been buying us? We can and must do better.

The case for reform, for opening up a system that has become wasteful, self-serving, unwieldy, in a way corrupt, could not be more resounding. Our schools are not educating our young as they ought to be educated or meeting the requirements of many parents.

What should be done? The crucial step must be to end the virtual monopoly that the public (including separate) education system holds. As long as it is in a monopoly position as the sole recipient of taxation support, as long as it does not need to compete for its share of the student population, it will have no incentive to change or to provide better educational services to the public. Currently, it is no better than any bureaucracy protecting its privileged turf. Insiders and defenders of the public school system argue that it is capable of responsiveness to the community, for example, Jane Dobell in the *Ottawa Citizen* symposium referred to earlier.[3] However, she views better service as catering to greater diversity of needs, not explicitly the provision of higher standards of education. They are not at all the same. Indeed, all three articles seem preoccupied with the issue of public support for schools sponsored by religious groups or denominations.[4] This is an issue, to be sure, a highly emotional one, but surely not the central one: the quality of education. I would argue that the public school system is incapable of improving quality in education without fair competition. It is too comfortable and protected, its funding too automatic, its energies and creativity too dissipated. The public education system is like the giant corporation of the 1950s, strong on volume, weak on quality, catering hitherto to a growing market prepared to take what it can get. But times have changed, and like the 1950s corporation, the education system has to change with them.

But how is competition to be introduced? Let us start with the position already outlined for managing enterprises, namely, that the role of government is to set standards and ensure excellence in education, not to run a school system. Raising standards alone will take most of the shrinking resources, the energy, and the commitment that governments possess. It is a task they are not performing at all adequately now.[5] They will need to show much greater openness to models from elsewhere like the IB. Canadian educators must give up their terrible smugness and begin to learn again. And, while not ignoring the social context of education, they must stop treating schools as primarily social welfare institutions. Just as we overload the tax system with two many functions when we try to do three or four major things with it, so we overload, and undermine, the school system when we try to make it do too many things.

The running of schools, if not monopolized by public municipal boards, will then fall to both municipalities and private educational entrepreneurs. Equal treatment of all schools – the creation of a "level playing field" – will require one of at least three approaches to funding:

1. Tax dollars could be shared among all schools – public or private – that meet provincial standards;
2. schools could be funded entirely privately, through fees paid direct to them by parents (and provincial and municipal taxation for education reduced accordingly);
3. current taxation could remain in place and parents be provided with "vouchers" that can be used at qualifying schools of their choice to pay tuition.

Each of these well-known options deserves careful study but a few brief remarks may help in sorting through them.

Option 2 is probably unacceptable to most Canadians. It gives the maximum freedom of choice to some parents, but it is the most at odds with the principle of equality of opportunity. Those with the resources would be able to afford a better education for their children than those without. There would be a hierarchy of quality in education based on wealth. Today's private schools that are primarily for the social elite would sit at the acme of the system, but they would be inaccessible to the vast majority because of cost. Some lower income earners might have insufficient funds to pay tuition charges: indeed, as the taxes they now pay to municipal authorities might be lower than the cost of tuition in an all-private system, they might experience a net loss in this sort of regime. Of course, since many poor people or people without salary or other private income would have to receive assistance, there might need to be a special welfare category created to pay for the education of their children. But, even then, Canadians would resist so loose and unfair an alternative, one that creates a class system in education.

Option 1, direct funding of both public and private schools from the public purse, is likely to be favoured by governments since it would allow them to maintain the maximum control. The power of the purse is always formidable. Assuming a school's enrolment would determine the size of provincial grants, there presumably would be a measure of market regulation because popular schools would command greater financial support. However, I would be concerned about the probably slow response to demand. The biggest game in town – handing over money – would be a matter between institutions, shutting parents out in the cold. There would be a great deal of room for government bureaucracy, or for a back-room process connecting bureaucrats and schools, to stymie or obstruct the wishes of individual parents. How would new schools make themselves eligible for funding?

There is also the question of whether all private schools should receive support. I do not believe that they should. If the existing, established private schools, many of which cater to the highest end of the income scale, receive public support, their budgets will be all the fatter and their advantage over other schools all the greater. Something like this has happened in Quebec. Coming late to the concept of public education, Quebec decided in the 1960s to provide funding to all schools that met its curriculum standards. Of course, many of these were the broadly based Catholic and Protestant/Jewish systems, but, as I understand it, the elite schools were among those receiving support too. However, the object of radical education reform is not to increase the competitive advantage of privileged schools and privileged families. We need to think in terms of a quite different kind of "private" school whose doors are open to everyone. I will expand on the idea in a moment. But, if public funding is provided to only some schools, how are provincial education departments to make the distinction? How are they to decide which schools to fund and which not to fund? Schools may have to choose between public funding and private funding. "Extra billing" ought, perhaps, to be disallowed.

Option 3, education vouchers, avoids most of the pitfalls and is the most responsive to clients' needs. It would leave sufficient power in the hands of government to ensure its role as setter of standards and as ultimate protector, in extreme cases, of the rights of children. It would maximize the freedom of choice of parents. It would ensure equality of opportunity regardless of a family's wealth; and, through competition, it would promote higher standards and better service to the public. Only those schools would receive financial support that attracted paying students.

No solution is a catch-all and many issues would have to be resolved. Once again, there is the issue of established private schools that have substantial funds of their own. Jane Dobell rightly argues that public support for private schools should not merely subsidize pricey private schools, reducing the cost to parents who can afford to pay or giving middle class parents the opportunity to upgrade. Schools that are funded from private tuition payments, in cash and endowments, would remain fully private. They could continue to exist to serve their wealthy clientele and meet or exceed provincial standards as they wish. They would still make a contribution to the competitive environment and the achievement of excellence. By the way, this does not mean that schools should not be profit-making. Cost-effectiveness should be the objective; profitability should not come into it. If a school can make something out of its voucher payments, while still not charging extra, all the better. That would be a reasonable financial incentive for them.

Another important consideration is that Option 1 or 3 not end up being more costly than the existing system. People who are not members of the community, such as foreign students, would have to be self-supporting. Finally, a voucher system should not collapse into a form of Option 1. There should be no delay in cash transfers, no bureaucratic process for payment, as long as a school meets provincial standards. Vouchers must be like money, instantly cashable by a qualified school once fees have been "paid."

What would be the benefits of such a system? First, there would be a strong financial incentive, for both enterprising teachers within the public system and outsiders, to establish schools and "sell" alternative curricula and teaching methods to parents and students. Since freedom of choice would devolve upon families, such schools would have to provide them with services they were satisfied with – and at reasonable cost – or they would not survive. There would be a good deal of competition for a share of the pie and some unevenness and disorder during the transition, but competition should keep costs under better control. Since many parents would demand higher quality education for their children, the likelihood would be strong that some of the new schools would provide such quality. That would be good for the system as a whole, with many schools competing for the best students and for the best reputations. Of course, the public authorities in the provincial departments would need to abandon their levelling mentality and take on excellence as a fundamental objective.

The public system itself would no doubt survive and should benefit from competition. It would shrink considerably, of course, but it would have an opportunity to retool and offer very much better services to the public than it does now.[6] It would have tremendous assets as the successor of the current system, the one that has long cornered the market and that possesses substantial resources. The reform I envisage will have failed if the public system turns into a useless backwater. One is reminded of the British system, in which there is a sort of class distinction – I mean in terms of quality of education, not social class alone – between the traditional "public," that is, private, schools and the state-run system. That would not be an improvement on our current system and it is certainly not what the great majority of Canadians would tolerate.

Of course, there would be fly-by-nighters who would try to take advantage of the wide open situation. This is where governments come in: they would need to be decisive in enforcing standards and ruthless in removing certification from schools that do not measure up – and stop penalizing achievement that exceeds standards. At the same time, they would need to focus on results, on ends and not means. Whether a school achieves bona fide standards at each level and produces graduates with the proper skills is what is important.

Such a mixed system would result in considerable diversity. Diversity, primarily means a variety of approaches to education; the education system should be able to accommodate Montessori, for instance, perhaps Waldorf (the experimental system invented by Austrian theorist Rudolf Steiner and present in a number of our communities), certainly IB and the *lycée* system, and curricula that deal with special needs. In Canada diversity also involves the language of instruction, in particular French, English, or both. Newer, more experimental approaches would be encouraged. Jane Dobell argues that the public school system is capable of offering greater diversity and responsiveness to needs and demands and is already doing so. However, it stands to reason that an open market system will do this better. Our current systems, including the vast bureaucracies in provincial capitals, are cumbersome, cautious, smug, and slow. Moreover, there may be an argument for less diversity in the public school system. Greater diversity has been one of the causes of dilution of standards; our public schools have sought to be all things to all people. Perhaps they should occupy a niche, indeed the middle ground, the mainstream, and allow specialists outside the public system to concentrate on special needs.

To many people, however, diversity implies cultural diversity and difference of religious persuasion. Special groups might insist on having their own state-supported schools. Every educated person's fear is that a fundamentalist group might gain control of a local board, as has been threatened in the United States, and bump something that offends them, evolution for instance, off the curriculum. A major new development is that increasing numbers of Canadians now come from non-Christian backgrounds and have values sometimes at odds with those of mainstream Canada. There is no question that this entire area is a minefield, but governments must not shrink from their responsibility as standards-setters. There should be no funding for religious instruction; this lies outside the mandate of the public purse and must remain a private matter. Moreover, religious schools that do not adhere to, and teach, the minimum standard curriculum would receive no support. There must be no compromise with anti-intellectual and unscientific doctrines like Creationism, for example. Religious groups are free to teach whatever they want but have no right to funding for a non-standard curriculum. Beyond these concerns, there seems to me no reason to worry about cultural diversity in the system, even if a grouping is new or distasteful to average Canadians. In fact, nearly all the established religious groups already run private schools. Of course, they would have the option of remaining wholly private and privately funded if they chose.

So strikingly novel and unsettling are these ideas to many Canadians that resistance to them is inevitable. The public system itself will be particularly resistant to change because its power, its monopoly, the comfort of its managers and workers, perhaps even its existence, would be at stake. Some will complain about the difficulties of transition. Resistance among teachers could be strong and destabilizing for a time, though "industrial action" would again be rather like the action of Cargill's miners, trying to lock the door against change and undermining their own future by failing to adapt to it. The transition needs to be planned carefully and with minimum disruption. At the same time, novelty should not be waylaid or penalized.

Mostly, however, I suspect that resistance will be psychological, the inevitable scepticism about the unfamiliar, a failure, or a refusal, to believe that education can be anything but public. This attitude lies behind halfway-house positions I have seen expressed in the media. Recognizing the need for change and for offering alternatives to the current more or less monolithic system, some are attracted by the option of autonomous community schools, "charter schools," run much more independently by local parents, tailoring their curricula to local needs or to the special wishes of the parents. This may indeed be a viable option. On the other hand, it assumes a broad uniformity of choice within a community and it could prove very restrictive in small communities. Individual parents may still dissent and be interested in other options. In the *Citizen* symposium, Bernard Shapiro argues for "associate schools," private, independent schools that meet stringent public criteria but offer wider diversity of choice to parents and "associate" themselves with public school boards in order to share administration, a core curriculum, and public funding. This seems to me a good option, especially in its emphasis on shared support, but not as good, as flexible, or as liberal as a voucher system. It is effectively Option 1, as described.

More broadly, the educational system should be able to admit under its umbrella a variety of management forms. But, as with privatization of government enterprises or parts of the welfare system, we should not be deterred by terms like "private" or "profit" if private, profit-making enterprises can deliver the goods. Private schools in a new, more open, more diverse system will not be like private schools today, nor will they relate to public schools in the same way. Drucker calls them "accountable schools," in that they will be much more directly accountable to parents than schools we have today.[7] The object is a better education for our children within an affordable fiscal framework. In the absence of such a reform, we will fail to arrest a decline not only in education but in our society and economy as a whole.

CHAPTER SEVEN

EFFICIENCY IN THE PUBLIC SERVICE

Government will always be wasteful and will always be a net burden on the economy unless and until its operational processes can be as productive as those of other organizations in society. Sceptic or not, you have to try to improve the way governments do their business. Not to try is to abandon the field and allow even those responsibilities government is bound to have to retain to be done badly. There is no reason why you and I, who pay for the services of government, should not be as demanding regarding them as we are when we purchase services on the open market. But the question persists: how can government be made more productive and more efficient?

To answer this question, one must start by getting clearer the nature of public service and how it differs from the private sector. Many argue that efficiency cannot be attained in the public service in quite the same ways as it can in a private business because of unbridgeable differences between them. One must also make some distinctions among different types of activities performed by the public sector, because the way government does its business cannot be improved in the same way everywhere.

The crux of public service theory for many important and intelligent public servants is summed up by Clerk of the Privy Council Mademoiselle Bourgon, as follows: "We must guard against the simplistic notion that the public sector should be run like a private enterprise." What does this mean?

Basically, it means that government does not serve a customer but all customers, the public as a whole. Its object is not to make a profit out of its customers but to provide them with common services based on a fair and equitable standard. No one would quarrel with this – at least, I do not. But we must examine it carefully and separate its essential meaning from harmful ways in which it may be interpreted, wheat from chaff. What is essential to public administration and what limitations does it impose on the way public funds may be administered?

First, the Public Service is, and always must be, accountable through ministers to Parliament, and through Parliament to the people themselves. The public service cannot use funds in a way contrary to what Parliament and the law prescribe.

Secondly, government must indeed treat all citizens and other legal residents with scrupulous fairness. Everyone shares the same rights as a member of the polity and for this reason alone. Government must therefore implement its policies blindfolded, like Justice. There may be legitimate questions about the rights of some who are peripheral to the polity (for example, the right to government assistance of those who are not legal permanent residents) but we can find no grounds for discriminating against legal residents in the application of the law or of universal government programmes.

Thirdly, governments serve all of the people. Consequently, the notion of the "customers" of governments is a hard one to apply. In some instances, a government process really is customer-oriented and its customers are a limited, clearly defined group. For example, exporters seeking trade promotion services, buyers of passports or researchers looking for information in governmental hands.

In many instances virtually all Canadians are (or become) the customers of a government programme, such as recipients of social security and medical insurance benefits. Perhaps law-enforcement agencies should be included, in that all law-abiding citizens are "customers" who receive protective services from them. In these instances, the concepts of "customers" and "public" become virtually identical. Nevertheless, the customer concept fits these cases aptly and adds something that the notion of "the public interest" by itself does not capture. It portrays certain governmental activities as processes that provide products or services to people and in this respect emphasizes a feature that parts of the public sector and all of the private sector have in common.

Other services, like regulatory agencies, tax collectors, and policy departments are much harder to fit into the "customer" mould. I have offered a number of examples of each of these already. Typical regulatory agencies at the federal level abound in, or in association with, Environment Canada, Transport Canada and Heritage Canada. By "policy" departments I mean something a little broader than the central agencies, which are the chief policy organs of the government. I mean departments whose policies flow into operations that are viewed as being in the public interest, but that do not involve direct services to clients, for example, those who conduct foreign relations, the military, security and intelligence authorities, drafters of laws, and so on. They are said to serve the public as a whole but are all of the people their customers? If we say yes, the concept becomes stretched out of recognition.

Are those whom regulatory bodies oversee their customers? Of course, they may be willing partners. Self-regulation is to be encouraged. Socially responsible companies recognize the broader interests of their customers in clean air, health and safety. Just as the law-abiding may be viewed as clients of the law enforcement agencies, those who abide by regulations may be considered as customers of regulatory agencies. Moreover, these activities can, up to a point at least, be run as services, in the sense that agencies can guide companies and the general public in the best and most cost-effective ways to comply with rules. Punishment is the wrong way to treat the just. The discussion in Chapter Four foreshadowed these remarks. Every subject of regulation deserves to be treated with courtesy, not as an adversary. But regulators will always be enforcers up to a point, especially in the case of wilful or persistent rule-breakers. They need to keep a certain distance and be prepared to use a stick if necessary. Their clientele cannot always be viewed as customers. Much the same may be said of tax collection.

In policy-driven bureaucracies, indeed in the policy functions of all departments, activity tends to flow upwards, away from customers – if they have any. Departments have a policy guidance role in relation to their ministers. However good the theory that ministers are the chief servants of the public, ministers will always be like generals commanding huge armies; both the pressure of work and their own power mean that their departments will have to spend a good deal of time and money (time is money) meeting ministerial needs and wishes. The public does not come as a customer to policy agencies. Policy agencies are remote from real people and the public interest is an abstraction for them.

The realization of service to the public by such bodies is an unsolved problem in the theory and practice of public administration, and it is not a trivial problem. How is the public interest really served by such bodies? What are the standards for such service? How do you measure it? Sometimes, policy development is a means of supporting a client-driven process, but not all policy bodies – and none of the central agencies – can be understood in this way. I do not wish to trivialize the policy enterprise. The real function of policy is not simply to assist ministers but to inform and direct operations. Policy ought to flow downwards. You have to get policy right. If you do not, little that government does will be to our benefit. This may be the sense, then, in which the policy agencies serve the public, but the service they provide is at a distance and exceedingly difficult, if not impossible, to measure.

Now for the chaff. What is not implied by the central tenets of public service theory? What should we refuse to accept as essential to it?

The special nature of public service does not mean that customer-oriented government bureaucracies are immune from the requirement to run lean, efficient operations that are the equal in productivity and efficiency of those in the private sector, or to provide as swift and thorough service to the public as in the private sector.

Accountability to Parliament does not mean that departments must confound themselves with multiple systems of control and tangled nets of useless rules that turn their administration into costly nightmares. The purpose of control is to account for money, but surely in the interest of saving it and ensuring it is well spent. Most control mechanisms now cost vastly more than they save. This is a transparent example of policy becoming detached from its essential purposes.

Departments provide services to ministers but they are not therefore purely upward-looking pyramids. If they are service- or production-oriented, they must serve their customers efficiently. Efficient, streamlined departments serve a minister's principal need, which is to serve his or her national constituency.

Governments must be fair, in following procedures for contract bids, for example, but that does not justify practices so obstructive that they make government-private sector contracting barely liveable for a private contractor doing business with government, or make the contracting-out process too cumbersome to result in real offloading. Yet, this is what continues to be the rule.

There are indeed pertinent differences between the public and the private sectors and they will give some distinctive character to the way public administration operates, but there is no philosophical or theoretical reason why the lion's share of public administration can still not be run as efficiently as a business. However they are intended, remarks about the differences often merely confirm many public servants in their belief that it is acceptable for public institutions to be less efficient than the private sector, that it is "natural" for them to be so, that it is part of their essence.

Management and administration exist to direct government to carry out its functions properly and to support operations. They are overhead. They do not exist for their own sake. The internal services they provide can be measured and evaluated. They need to set a good example by being lean and mean themselves. There is no excuse for the current situation in which the overhead of government is its largest single operational expense, as I understand it is calculated to be.

The main obstacles to radical improvements in efficiency in the public service remain the inertia of the system, fear of the turmoil into which radical change would tend to lead personnel, the lack of real public accountability (organizations go on existing even if they waste resources, do a bad job and displease customers) and the lack of incentives to induce managers to reduce public expenditure and eliminate waste. Yet, the first two of these apply as much to the private sector as to the public and the last two, while endemic to government, are hardly part of anyone's ideal of public service.

What is to be done?

There are scores of books about how to improve the efficiency of organizations, thousands of consultants who make their living from it and much knowledge and activity even in government. I will touch lightly on the subject by discussing only a few ideas, not for the benefit of the many who know already about these things, but for the benefit of the many more who do not. There is no panacea, but there are sensible practices that can be adopted. In Canada, at least at the federal level, efforts to bring about change are numerous but they have been haphazard at best and have barely scratched the surface of the bureaucracy as a whole.

I would like to discuss first a concept that applies to all government agencies, including the elitist and least customer-driven ones. It is exceedingly simple but it has in the main been followed almost nowhere. For lack of a better term, it may be called strategic management or priority-driven management. Ever since I began to work as a public servant, the notion of "management by objectives" has held sway. Goals and objectives may be key to effective management, but the process of management by objectives has consistently been wasteful and misdirected. It led to "strategic planning" in the form of producing vast tomes of goals and strategies that few people paid much attention to, that bore limited relation to real operations, and that changed marginally from year to year. These were "good times" documents belonging to a time when there were funds availabe to expand government. Planning outfits became independent organizational units competing with, rather than supporting, operations. What was missing from these practices were simplicity, a willingness to change and save resources on behalf of the Canadian taxpayer, a focus on priorities, coordination of these in a vision of where the organization wishes to go, results orientation (that is, a focus on the outputs of processes rather than the inputs or the processes themselves), effective performance measurement and staff buy-in or support.

Most of this sounds like jargon and it is or has become so. It is important to concentrate on the real meaning behind it. What is envisaged is a dynamic management process that does the following six tasks.

ESTABLISH VISION

The leadership's vision is its concept of what they want their organization to be. It is the framework for its goals. When Henry Ford envisaged an affordable car in front of every home and the nature of the organization he would need to achieve this, his was a powerful vision, one that transformed the whole automobile industry and much of modern life. When Transport Canada sees itself as a streamlined policy department that establishes the guidelines for airport management but gets out of the business of running airports itself, it has a vision of itself as an organization very different from what it has been for decades. This is a goal, to be sure, but one of a special kind. It is the goal that gives rise to a set of more specific goals and strategies designed to realize the vision. A vision is simple and challenging, but achievable. It can be a powerful motivator for staff. Think of Wal-Mart and Amway and their very different visions of the type of quality and service needed to capture the same market.

SET PRIORITIES

Management as the core corporate body establishes the goals of an organization, nearly always for a year. It must also establish priorities among these goals and, in light of the available resources, decide which of them will be implemented.

ABANDON LOW-PRIORITY LINES

By the same token, it must decide which of the organization's business lines have had their day and should be abandoned in favour of more important new ones or to provide savings to the taxpayer. This sounds, and is, the only logical way to keep an organization fresh and its programmes current, low in cost, and of value to the public, but virtually no governmental organization I know of has done this consistently – at least not before the current era of Programme Review. Virtually all find it dreadfully hard to let anything go.

DEFINE OBJECTIVES CLEARLY

Objectives were, and are, frequently written with exemplary vagueness so that no blame can be laid for a failure to reach them. At a minimum, goals must be expressed so that management can tell whether targets have been hit or not. In the cases where it is possible, they should be quantifiable.

GIVE PRIORITIES TO A SLEEK STAFF OF STRATEGIC PLANNERS

Strategic planning, as an instrument of this type of management, has a clear and relatively straightforward job. It refines the priorities handed down by management, ensures they are conceptually sound and works out strategies to achieve them. To be real-life, strategic planning must flow into strategic finance, resource planning, budget-making and, as Peter Drucker says, work. The priorities must be embodied in real work and resource decisions. In how many departments today is the budget driven by the strategic or business plan? This is a powerful tool in ensuring responsiveness of independent kingdoms in organizations to central management direction.

MEASURE RESULTS

Clear targets engender measurable results. Performance measurement is not, or should not be, the measurement of the flow of work but of its results. It should not be a burden (as old-fashioned strategic planning and audit often were) but an aid. Indeed, it is an essential function. Performance measurement informs management which of its goals were reached and which were not, or, were only partially achieved. For those goals not achieved, it poses the question, Why not? Next year's priorities can hardly be set wisely without this information nor can economical, useful audit or review be accomplished; yet, few government organizations do real performance measurement now.

I have used the term "simplicity" several times. Simplicity is important not only to ensure understanding and to motivate people, it is an essential element of policy that governments are very prone to ignore. The point I wish to make ties into some of the early discussions in this essay. Many government programmes have unclear and complicated objectives. They are overloaded with goals, some of them contradicting other goals. I used the tax system as a particularly pertinent example. Perhaps, as a friend of mine suggests, there should be one programme or delivery instrument for each goal. At the very least, the goals of a programme need to be clear, rational, small in number, and consistent with one another. The policy functions of government have a lot to clean up. This alone may justify some of the resources we devote to them.

Bits and pieces of the strategic approach have been found in government, but it has been honoured most often in the breach. The "zero-based budgeting" concept that has been recommended to government agencies embodies it in a number of respects. It involves starting each year from scratch. All programmes are terminated and new ones must be built up and resources obtained for them on the basis of new justifications and new priorities each year. The Japanese model is called "slash and build." This ought to be a powerful instrument for budget reduction, but it is almost never practised. Government budgets have nearly always been based on last year's, and programmes are viewed as never-ending – unless doomsday comes.

Programme Review was an effort to apply principles like these but on a one-time crisis-centered basis. It pointed in all the right directions, but given the speed with which it was carried out, it was bound to be superficial. Small wonder that many observers saw it in the end as a cover for the Finance Department's axe. Treasury Board's new expenditure management system looks finally like the means of turning these concepts into standard ones for managing agencies and controlling their expenditures annually, imposing, for example, a virtual no-growth condition, but the schema remains rudimentary and untried. The government is at best a year away from developing a business-line model for expenditure to replace the current, archaic one. The current one is based on categories of expenditure – or pots of money – for things like travel, supplies, capital expenditure, and salaries. A business-like model puts together all the financial resources needed for a single "business," like delivering old age pensions to clients. This concept should become clearer a little later this chapter. And, the biggest obstacle of all, the plan will be implemented by a bureaucracy whose "culture" is radically at odds with the new concepts and that has enormous capacity to mangle or obstruct it.

Another effort to put clothes on some of these concepts is the Special Operating Agency (SOA) concept. It seeks, in addition, to give certain service-providing organizations, whether at departmental or sub-departmental level, greater freedom from Treasury Board rules. The SOA will probably survive and be used, but a sign of the vulnerability of such mechanisms was the trouble the Canada Communications Group got into early this year, when it was viewed to be helping departments circumvent annual budgeting. The whole concept was put on ice for review and no new SOAs have, to my knowledge, been created since. Government has great difficulty living with the consequences of its own risks.

The power and effectiveness of effecting reform through better, sounder, conceptually clearer and more rational approaches has been demonstrated by Australia since the late 1980s. Without any radical reform of the bureaucratic process – indeed, while maintaining a philosophy of public service that is downright conservative in its stress on traditional public service values – Australia has pulled itself out of a fiscal nightmare, established clear and firm principles of management, turned chronic budgetary growth and bureaucratic infighting into careful management of resources, and achieved annually small, but incrementally significant savings. Out-of-control foreign indebtedness has been brought back under control and the public debt as a whole has been reduced to about 20 per cent of GDP. During the same period, we in Canada were touting a comparable theory under the title Public Service 2000, almost none of which we implemented or took seriously outside the management classrooms.

Strategic management is the sine qua non of better government practices. Without the right policies, as I have said, the best and most efficient operations will be without meaning or justification. Strategic management is of particular importance when the blank sheet, the need to design whole new approaches to an area, becomes essential. Take the area of communications policy. We are in the midst of a technological revolution of untold proportions. It will affect the way every type of electronic transmission is delivered to us. The shape of the world to come is emerging in "The Information Superhighway," the Internet technology and multimedia computer technology. The distinctions between communications and databases, between radio/TV and interactive, digitally based communication, among the telephone, the video set, and the computer, are all becoming blurred. The policies and strategies adopted by our governments on this field over the next few years will be of the utmost importance in ensuring that the practices of both the private and public sectors will serve the public interest for many years to come.

Improving the processes of government without first ensuring strategic direction will be of only marginal value. It may save some money but at great cost, since doing the wrong things well is of no value. Nevertheless, if the right strategic framework is in place, it is critical to improve the efficiency of programmes and processes, to make them more effective in serving clients and to reduce their cost. A number of tools exist to achieve these ends. They are being applied widely outside government and are steadily being refined. But the bureaucracy lags in understanding, adopting, and applying them. It is rather better at misunderstanding and distorting them, pretending that it was doing the right things all along. The adoption of these tools by government is of great importance in doing something about the ugly and wasteful practices and the top-heavy structures that were described in the opening chapters of this essay.

The central insights of these theories revolve around the notion of the business process. Most of us are accustomed to using the word "business" for private industry, the opposite of government. That is not the sense in which the term is used here. A business is any product or service line, whether public or private sector. Governments are involved in all kinds of businesses. This is not a misapplication of the word, one more misbegotten effort to assimilate government to private industry. Although the concept of business process has something of a history, it has come to be associated with two strands of contemporary management theory in particular, Total Quality Management (TQM) and Business Process Re-engineering (BPR).[1] The former is identified with W. Edwards Deming, the latter with Michael Hammer and James Champy.[2] The concept of business process improvement is key; thus, I will usually speak of "business process redesign." However, I am going to make primary use of BPR theory because it sets out the issues and solutions in particularly arresting terms. Indeed, I owe my own understanding of the critical insights to Hammer and Champy.

In a paper to which I have just referred in a note, Ole Ingstrup, principal of the Canadian Centre for Management Development, belittles Hammer and Champy for extravagant claims, for "hype." He is right to show some scepticism and challenge hyperbole. Certainly it is unwise to get carried away by enthusiasm. Management theories must be understood thoroughly and implemented rationally. However, "hype" has its uses, though not to experts like Ingstrup. Most of the Public Service lags embarrasingly in its grasp of process theory. The management training and informal instruction I, as an operational manager in a policy-dominated department, encountered between 1990 and 1993 – mostly from Public Service 2000 and indirectly from TQM – made no impact on me. I had no understanding of the meaning, or appreciation of the importance, of the business process concept until I encountered BPR, and then, with much more effect, read the Hammer/Champy book. Hammer and Champy and many other management consultants are also performers, but so are many prominent educators. "Hype" makes an impact at the beginning of the educational process. It may serve as an effective teaching tool.

Hammer and Champy define BPR as the radical redesign of business processes with the aim of improving efficiency and productivity, as well as save money – savings of two-, three- or fourfold, or even more. Debates rage about whether reengineering can be applied to government and Sceptics also point to its hit-or-miss impact even in the private sector. It is not without risks and it needs to be applied with great care and precision.

BPR claims to be radical, to go back to a blank slate and redesigning a process from scratch. Whether this is necessary depends on circumstances, but, whether rapid or gradual change is preferred, the result is indeed a thorough transformation of the way business is done. Literal reengineering is, let us say, completely redesigning an automobile, so that it will be better, more economical, less costly, and able to compete with the high-quality products coming out of Japan and the cheaper cars coming out of other newly industrialized countries. Reengineering of industrial processes is the remodelling not of the vehicle, but of the assembly line that produces it. Multidisciplinary teams made up of appropriate specialists produce whole cars. They do not install only ball bearings, or wheels or fenders or some other component, and pass the would-be vehicle on to someone else for the next step. Applied to the white-collar world, reengineering is an assault on the pyramidal bureaucratic structure described in Chapter Two.[3]

Hammer and Champy term the traditional bureaucracy the "Adam Smith" organization, since it is based on the principle of the division of labour that Smith discovered. He observed in the incipient factories of his day how division of labour led to a manifold leap in productivity over household craft industry. Workers considered too stupid to manufacture something whole could be readily trained to do simple repetitive functions quickly, producing standardized parts that someone else in the chain was tasked, under stern managerial eyes, to fit into their proper place in the end-product. The industrial revolution adopted this model and eventually turned it into the full-fledged, mechanized assembly line, but bureaucracies have adopted it too. In the classic bureaucracy, a unit is trained to do or check one operation, then pass it to the next for another operation.

The division-of-labour approach in bureaucracies has four major shortcomings. The first is that workflow is divided into small tasks, so that processes are truncated and bifurcated, involving many hands, much delay, and significant potential for error. The second is that great amounts of time, money and energy must be devoted to what is called "liaison" (I had trouble believing there was such a verb as "liaise" until I began to work for government, but lo, it is in the dictionary), checking with all the cooks who have their fingers in the soup to make sure everyone is "on side." This process is always costly and, all too frequently, it brings activity to a standstill. The alternative, go-it-alone action without consultation, produces either serious conflict and paralysis, or duplication and chaos, government speaking and acting with many, frequently contradictory, voices. The third problem is that a hierarchical organization is required to coordinate all this fractionalized effort and work out snags. You have to have section heads, directors, and more senior managers above them to put the process, like Humpty Dumpty, back together again. The energy of the whole production line is dissipated by movements up and down the chain of command to obtain approvals and direction. A fourth problem is that the bits-and-pieces work handed down to the workers is unchallenging and demoralizing. The division of labour causes people-problems in organizations.

Reengineering and TQM draw attention to the need to reunite divided processes into whole ones. This is where a number of critical concepts of the business process and business process redesign come in. Seven elements go into this.

1. Identifying processes correctly: most processes cut across traditional organizational boundary lines. Checking addition is not a process; budget management may be the process. Uniting processes breaks down the turf and hierarchical barriers that currently stymie them. It also identifies components of a process that are useless and can be bypassed and abolished.
2. Customer-orientation: crucial to defining a process is identifying its end, the customer for whom a product or service is provided. Because reengineering is about efficient and effective service to customers, it is applicable, in the main, only to those agencies of government that serve cus-

tomers or produce a product for customers. Some of its elements, however, might help improve efficiency in other types of processes, such as internal services (logistics).

3. Teams: ideally, a process should be run by an integrated team that contains all or almost all of the resources needed to achieve its aim. Often one person, a customer relations officer, oversees an entire project or "case." The process is not divided up into boxes.
4. Flattening the organization: most of the layers disappear. Middle management, especially, is no longer needed. Responsibility is diffused among a wider body of staff.
5. Leadership: leadership becomes more important than direction or systems management. The number of managers is reduced considerably; their role becomes more focused on larger issues such as resources, planning, and working out special problems, not day-to-day tasking and monitoring of work.
6. Responsibility: the driving force of the organization rests in the teams and responsibility and decision-making are thrust downward to them. This is usually called "empowerment."
7. Information technology: virtually every part of the new way of doing business depends on state-of-the-art information technology, which puts the needed information and automated tools in the hands of the teams. This eliminates many component activities now done by people.

But is any of this applicable to government? Is the "uniqueness" of the public sector such that theories developed for the private sector cannot apply? Although most government operations can be viewed as processes, not all fit easily into the mould of business processes. Policy-dominated processes, for example, differ from business processes in having no readily identifiable clients. Advisory functions look upward to ministers, away from real clients. I have had cause to belabour this point already.[4] Take foreign relations as an example: there are Canadians interested in our relations with country X, but it is not always, maybe not often, possible to qualify them as clients. Still less are the governments or the people of foreign countries our clients. Policy and strategic management inform business processes, give them their direction and shape, and therefore should not be confused with the processes themselves. On the other hand, some efficiency tools identified in redesign may have an application to the policy and management functions. Managerial ingenuity and empirical testing will tell us how.

However, there are a great many governmental operations that can be assimilated closely to the business process model. They are production or service lines with clients. They can make use of practically any tool to improve efficiency that is available to the private sector. But the application of TQM or BPR will produce changes that are bound to cause resistance.

Team approaches, which are the best means of organizing around business processes, are anti-hierarchical. They make the middle management layer obsolete, or merge it with team leadership at the front line serving customers. Team approaches also break down many walls between operational and support units. Specialists – technical, administrative, financial, and so on – who previously sat in separate divisions removed from the service end of the pipe may be integrated into the teams. The means would have to be found to retain professional identity and expertise, since the need for specialists will increase even as the need to focus them on the overall goals of a business process becomes paramount. Of course, it may not always be advisable for specialists to be fully integrated into operational process teams. It may be that a critical mass of them is required to maintain expertise and provide internal services. But even independent support elements can undergo process redesign similar to that of the operational teams. Their clients become internal clients. Serving an internal client does not automatically lead to better service for external clients. Connecting the two becomes a challenge for management.

Structure and authority would still be important in this radically slimmed down, flattened, streamlined organization but the number of managers would be reduced by a significant proportion. Senior managers would line up resources – financial and personnel – and focus them where they are required. They would be troubleshooters, solving special problems that the teams cannot solve. Naturally, they would develop the goals and priorities of the organization, and, with a planning staff, help translate them into doable work. Team leaders would lead and coordinate the teams on the front line dealing with customers. Essentially at the front end of the process, closest to customers, a team leader would coordinate inputs, resources, procurement activities, advice and the like needed to support the front line. However, teamwork is more important than the chain of command, and teams should be more versatile and multifaceted than traditional units. All team members are encouraged to assume responsibilities and take initiative. Senior managers would play a less hands-on role. They would need to establish accountability contracts with the junior management level, the team leaders. They would not minutely design or micro-manage the work of the teams. Team leaders are quite capable of doing this once they know their objectives. If you have heard that a boss must show he is boss by being able to do everyone's job in his organization better than the incumbents, do not believe it. No one can do that.

Budgetary, accounting, control, and personnel processes would need radical revision. No separate financial department, no gang of accountants, needs to look over the shoulders of managers, though an independent resource would probably still be necessary to help with budget design, to deal with basic financial administration (such as accounts payable) and to provide help and advice to others concerning rules and procedures. Control would not disappear but it would need to become much less obtrusive. On the one hand, one would have to do away with needless rules and rule-hounds. On the other, an independent, results-oriented function of audit or review hooked into a powerful financial database certainly ought to be part of the system. No one should assume that humans are better than they are: wrongdoing would be susceptible to discovery and redress.

Personnel policy poses a titanic obstacle. In many parts of the private sector, personnel policy has been greatly simplified. In one high-tech American company that produces virtually unique products at the high end of the scale in performance and price, there is a small number of personnel categories and a minimum number of grades within them. Not much time is wasted on promotion processes, which become routine and secondary. People are promoted on the basis of their experience and qualifications. But they are paid primarily for their effectiveness in obtaining results. Managers do not always get paid as much as professionals who have contributed handsomely to the company's success. Merit means results. Results in the Public Service are, of course, not a simple matter of making sales, enhancing profits, or inventing a new product line that does well. Nevertheless, it is more than possible to focus personnel policy on results, on what is achieved, rather than on what has traditionally constituted "performance" (the qualities that enable staff to be good citizens within a box-hierarchical structure). Paying people for what they achieve rather than for what they are is a key means of adopting such a focus. A "performance pay" concept quite different from the familiar one would need to be applied. The secret is the radical reduction of base pay, what one receives for level or for experience, and an increase in the merit pay factor substantially, to a range of, let us say, 50 per cent of the total. The appraisal process would focus practically all its prodigious energies not on promotion, but on measuring the effectiveness of staff and rewarding them accordingly. The importance of performance measures may once again be seen. Staff could have no better incentive than this, and there would be no more dramatic way of demolishing the sinecure syndrome in government.[5]

There is a very important people dimension to this. People are not only prone to resisting change. Some of the changes would be impossible for them to bear, especially where jobs are lost. All of this would need careful handling, both the altering of attitudes and the need for fair and gentle treatment of those most affected. At the same time, changes due to process redesign would not be greater – perhaps even less – than those now occurring as a result of Programme Review and budget reductions. They might be less because process redesign holds the promise of doing a job as well or better with fewer resources. Those engaged in streamlined processes are likely to be much more highly motivated and the savings generated might save important functions and processes elsewhere.

"Reinventing Government" is the phrase that has been used by the National Performance Review in the United States, an exercise that Vice President Gore took under his wing, and it, along with "reengineering," is gaining currency here, but to many it remains a foreign concept and is dismissed as a fad, or as inappropriate to the public sector.

Many of those who talk about reinventing government do not mean it. They mean at best minor improvements considerably less ambitious. Gradualism in the Public Service is most of the time another name for uncoordinated, non-strategic change. The then-new clerk of the Privy Council said in May 1994 that reinvention of government embodied three facets: customer service, living within our means, and "the fundamental responsibility of all government toward its citizens, that is, the creation and fair distribution of wealth."[6] The last is nothing more nor less than a restatement of the basic principle of the welfare state and it is fundamentally flawed: government creates virtually no wealth and should be concerned with equalizing opportunity, not wealth (but more of this later). Apart from the admitted centrality of customer service to reengineering, the three principles combined do not come close to either reengineering or to more gradual forms of business process redesign. Her remarks were at best a pale reflection of the failed experiment known as Public Service 2000.

Nevertheless, there are efforts going on to implement process redesign and experiment with BPR. At the federal level, interest takes three forms. One is the application of the concept to a major activity. The redesign of income security programmes around "one-stop shopping" services is the most significant example. A second is the redesigning of smaller processes (usually administrative or support), such as procurement, or processing of orders or applications. Under the knife to the extent that it is, the Department of National Defence has applied BPR to many of its infrastructure processes, a by no means inconsiderable enterprise. A third is the effort being undertaken in central agencies of government to define government's main processes and establish standards for reengineering them. I am thinking less of Massé's programme of Public Service renewal, or of Programme Review, than of the effort led by the Treasury Board to link reengineering of processes to development of a massive electronic network in the federal government. I should, however, add as a potential fourth the impact of the new expenditure management system I have referred to earlier. It envisages replacing strategic planning and traditional budget design by "business planning," whose eventual aim will be to cost "business lines," in effect business processes, so that their value can be better assessed and their place in the scheme of priorities more clearly established. This system will force organizations to think in terms of their processes and perhaps reorganize around them. Business process redesign as defined in the management theory literature will not automatically result, but an important step will have been taken.

But these are just a beginning. What is desperately needed is more experience with process redesign in government, casebooks detailing the results of redesign efforts and establishing benchmarks, models of success. Only then can a proper, empirically-based business process theory be written for government. That is the next critical step and the condition for more successful efforts.

CHAPTER EIGHT

Old Liberalism

I have suggested that a pragmatic redefinition of the role of government will, by the force of logic, drive us into the broader issues of political theory. Pragmatism is not enough. We must reopen questions of principle. Yet, if this is so, it is something to which most management theory is oblivious. The literature does not recognize this need nor do most practitioners of change in government. Among the handful of popular organizational theorists, only someone like Peter Drucker with his broad European educational background sets his analyses and prescriptions in this wider context. Is this merely a biographical accident? Why must we move beyond practical improvements to what are, or at one time were considered, philosophical issues?

Some of the reasons are evident already. In fact, I have stacked the deck by introducing a number of political judgments into the discussion. If, as the federal government's Programme Review is doing now, we ask basic questions about the businesses government should be in, we are reopening the fundamental question: what is government for? You cannot stop with the "affordability criterion." The government we cannot afford now we may be able to afford in the future, even though such a government may lead us back into financial crisis or be contrary to our deepest interests. Moreover, many of the tendencies and methods of governmental bureaucracies – their size, power and high-handedness, for example – need to be called thoroughly into question. Occasional, much publicized instances of arbitrariness aside, the assumptions that underlie our governments' taxing power and the welfare state, the focus on equality, and the wholesale right of infringement upon freedom that governments have assumed for themselves often go unchallenged.

Government bureaucracy as portrayed in Chapters Two and Three is, in a nutshell (pardon the cliché), an authoritarian institution even in a democratic system. It is a hierarchical power structure. If you were to extend this structure to the whole of society, as socialists used to propose, society would become authoritarian as well. We would live in a dictatorship, no matter how much voting was done, and no matter how much discussion took place in parliaments.[1] We do not live in a society of that kind, but we do live in one in which the authoritarian institutions that make up the permanent parts of governments occupy a huge proportion of our lives: providing about a fifth of the jobs and absorbing almost two-fifths of our income. The size and nature of our governing institutions force upon us a fundamental re-examination of the state of our democracy.

Even some of the elements that make for effectiveness in government raise broader issues of principle. I have briefly mentioned organizational vision. Vision is absolutely essential; it is the launching pad for the goals and priorities of a business process. If it is not to be a bland restatement of existing practice or ideology, it has to be ambitious, revolutionary, earth-shaking so as to give life and direction to an organization. In private business this raises no difficulty at all. To be the best damned producer of widgets is a laudable objective (assuming the moral neutrality of widgets) and can be a driving force in research, design, production, and marketing. In a government organization the issue is more complicated. I am struck, as I read the vision statements of departments and agencies, by their unclarity concerning the limits of their ambition and their authority. Governments are always cautious, of course, because they doubt their capacity to achieve their principal goals, so they draw attention to practical restraints on their actions and waffle accordingly. But what if they could really achieve all that their vision statements aspire to? Would they end up doing too much, playing too great a role in society, beyond what is good for us as citizens? Would they know their moral limits?

Governments would be quick to point out that, whatever the nature of their vision statements, departments and agencies are limited by their statutory mandates. The object of more farsighted goals for a government agency is to escape the straitjacket of mere compliance with rules. They are indeed limited by their mandates and they do need to be creative and flexible in the interests of more efficient and cost-effective service delivery. But the growth of governmental power has occurred quite regardless of legislation, driven by policy, the beliefs and ambitions of politicians and civil servants, and a host of other factors. Whether governments improve their delivery of services or not, whether they reduce their costs or not, we have no choice, analytically speaking, but to go beyond practical considerations to the more fundamental one of what power government ought to have.

For much of this century, political philosophy has been considered dead. We have, after all, a firmly entrenched democracy in Canada, and democracy is advancing all around the world. It is indisputably the best system, the most oriented toward the public interest and the protection of human rights. All we need to do, the view has been, is "fine-tune" democracy, promote its universal use and live out our lives, seek our happiness, within its embrace. This appeared to be the view of Francis Fukuyama, who proclaimed (at first in an article and then in a book) "The End of History" when large parts of the world, Eastern Europe and Latin America especially, adopted democratic forms. His thesis recalled political theorist Daniel Bell's announcement of "the end of ideology" over three decades ago, when trends in democratic and communist countries seemed to be converging. Both were premature.

Almost no one doubts in our society the superiority of (liberal) democracy, but the belief that we no longer need to be creative political thinkers is dead wrong. In fact, democracy has changed dramatically during our century, and it will not do to be unconscious of what has shifted under our feet. It will go on changing, and there will be nothing automatic or inevitable about the benefits we may expect to flow from it. I would like, therefore, to go back to the roots of democratic thought in the modern Western world and consider some of the ways it has been interpreted and transformed.

First, a disclaimer! My treatment will be broad-brush but some readers will find this chapter and the next two over their heads, abstract and impractical. Others will recognize all too quickly my inadequacies as a thinker and see the errors covered up by my broad brush. I do not claim any knowledge of contemporary political philosophy as such, a field that has undergone considerable change in the last twenty-five to thirty years. It overcame its mid-century inhibitions about addressing large moral and political issues, but it has become very difficult and highly technical. I have virtually no acquaintance with it and still less with economics. I hope that those who know better will point out my errors and shortcomings.

Although they are not identical concepts, going back to the beginning of democratic theory means understanding liberalism. That is true in the democratic tradition we have inherited from the British, a tradition begun, pretty much, by John Locke (1632–1704) and conveyed to us through the nineteenth century liberal philosopher John Stuart Mill (1806–73), among others.

The fundamental principle of classic liberalism is the maximization of individual liberty. The power and role of government are derivative and limited. That is, individual liberties are primary and government may assume only those powers freely granted to it by its subjects. The principle of the maximization of personal freedom is fundamental to liberalism: abandon it and the whole theory is turned upside down.

John Locke's *Two Treatises of Government* (1690) puts forward the basic concepts of freedom and the role of government that helped give birth to liberal democratic theory and still remain part of its core.[2] This undeniable fact is due not just to the brilliance and farsightedness of Locke himself, but to historical circumstance. Locke's political theory was developed in a revolutionary age in England, and about a century later, became embodied, to all intents and purposes, in the constitution, political system, and political culture of what was to become the most formidable and influential democratic state of the modern world: the United States of America.

Locke develops his theory of freedom, in particular the primacy of individual liberties, through what is known as contract theory. He employs the myth, or abstraction, known as the state of nature, in which all humans (Locke, of course, said and meant men) are equal and their freedoms are limited only by human reason, the bounds of nature, and the realities of jostling up against other humans with the same aspirations and desires. For example, two or more persons may want the same thing and come into conflict over it. This jostling produces insecurity and to minimize this insecurity these primitives "contract" with one another to form "civil society," in which individuals are civilized by the introduction of mutually beneficial structure and stability. Humans consent to give up some of their freedom for the greater good of mutual protection. Locke foresaw other benefits, or "conveniences,"[3] that society can provide as a result of the social contract, but the sphere of governmental action is very narrow for him, including, besides criminal law and foreign relations, little more than the regulation of property.[4] The crux of his position is that individuals consign certain powers, in particular for the maintenance of public order, to the civil or political or sovereign power – to government.

Locke differed from his illustrious predecessor, Thomas Hobbes (1588–1679), author of *Leviathan*, in viewing the natural man as less savage, more rational, less driven by desperation, to establish civil society. Locke conceived of the basic or fundamental rights as "natural rights" discoverable by reason. Hobbes had a more pessimistic view of human nature – in the state of nature – seeing it in terms of greed for wealth and power, envy and aggression. For him, almost anything that imposed order was better than this brutish existence. Thus, Locke pressed toward a vision of democracy, while Hobbes was prepared to tolerate any system that banishes the chaos of the state of nature – even absolutism – as long as it is shorn of medieval superstitions and constraints. Hobbes, therefore, was neither liberal nor democrat, though he contributed substantially to the theoretical development of liberals like Locke who followed him. Locke created new ideals. At the same time, he may be justly charged with viewing humanity through rose-coloured glasses. His natural man is not driven into civil society by desperation, but has the aplomb to reason his way into it. Although both philosophers were wary of the power of governments, Hobbes prepares us better for their lapses into brutality and tyranny. As a result, our aspirations in democracies tend to be Lockean, but we find in spite of ourselves coming back again and again to the poignancy of Hobbes's insights. We have done so frequently already in the pages that precede, in seeking to understand bureaucratic behaviour, for example. Hobbes is our "reality check."

Unlike Hobbes' sovereign power, Locke's is tightly circumscribed. Freedoms rightly and naturally reside with citizens except insofar as they consent to surrender them. Any government that acts arbitrarily or tyranically may be rightfully dissolved or overthrown by its subjects.

The basic rights due to all humans are life, liberty, and property, in revolutionary America idealized as "life, liberty and the pursuit of happiness." The right to property is a key one for Locke and a considerable part of the *Second Treatise* is devoted to the nature of property and its protection. "The supreme power cannot take from any man part of his property without his own consent … It is true, governments cannot be supported without great charge, and it is fit every one who enjoys his share of the protection should pay … for the maintenance of it. But still it must be with his own consent."[5] Locke was most concerned about the taxing power of governments whose authority was perpetual, such as absolute monarchs and hereditary oligarchies. He considered that "variable" legislatures, those consisting of representatives chosen from time to time by the people, would be less likely to seek to enrich themselves at the expense of citizens.

The revolutionary nature of this political philosophy for its time is obvious, as is its resonance in colonial America. The cry of "No taxation without representation!" from an outraged citizenry being taxed by a distant, unrepresentative parliament is straight out of Locke. Locke's political theory has never ceased to have a receptive audience or clear relevance where a transition from arbitrary rule is under way, as it is now in Russia and the countries of Eastern Europe.

The nineteenth century was the heyday of liberalism. It is not easy to identify pure theorists in the United States, in part because most of them were active in politics, in building up their own liberal democratic system. Its most notable theorists, people like Jefferson and Madison, were at the same time revolutionaries, active politicians, and eventually presidents. Among many liberal theorists in England, where changes less cataclysmic but just as profound were occurring, none stands out more than John Stuart Mill. I would like to say a few words about Mill, focusing especially on his work, *On Liberty* (1859).

Superficially, Mill was a very different type of thinker from Locke. He abjured contract theory and theories of "abstract" rights. He abandoned the scenario of the state of nature. Yet, as we read the main tenets of his political thought, we find these differences insignificant. Mill, one could say, "demythologized" Locke but held all of his main beliefs.[6] They are worth recounting because, in the midst of the Victorian rhetoric and sometimes dated argument of his essays, they form an elegant, transparent, and cogent liberal programme.

First, Mill was an individualist. He believed in the freedom and diversity of thought and its rightful extension into action. "Free scope should be given to varieties of character, short of injury to others."[7] To individuals accrue rights, which he defines as those of their basic interests, whether recognized by law or by tacit understanding, that the conduct of other individuals ought not to injure.[8] What are the limits of society's infringement of these rights and of its power over human liberty in general? "The sole end for which mankind are warranted, individually or collectively, in interfering with the liberty of action of any of their number, is self-protection" that is, "to prevent harm to others. His own good, either physical or moral, is not a sufficient warrant."[9]

Although Mill rejected the idea of an original state of nature, he bought some of the myth himself in the form of an idealized history of individuality.[10] He looked back to a time when individuality reigned supreme, indeed was too strong, and considered that it had been in decline since then. Indeed, he viewed individuality as stronger even when monarchies were universal in medieval times. "There has been a time when the element of spontaneity and individuality was in excess and the social principle had a hard struggle with it. The difficulty then was to induce men of strong bodies or minds to pay obedience to any rules which required them to control their impulses."[11] In *Representative Government* he puts the matter even more clearly. "A people in a state of savage independence, in which everyone lives for himself, exempt ... from any external control, is practically incapable of making any progress in civilization until it has learnt to obey. To enable [a government] to [make itself obeyed], the constitution ... must be nearly, or quite, despotic."[12] Thus, at the low end of the spectrum, Mill finds a place for a primitive social state reminiscent of Hobbes' state of nature and in need of a Hobbesian despot to whack it into shape.

By implication, up the ladder of civilization less and less government is required, but nothing being inevitable in history, Mill saw the decline of individuality as continuing into his own times, as social conformity increasingly drives out idiosyncrasy, creativity, and diversity. Individuality may once have imperilled social peace but now the reverse is true, he suggests. The paradox is that in primitive societies individuality is at once the most potent and the most subject to external compulsion, whereas in advanced ones governmental power is less needed to control behaviour but more pervasive.

The ideal role of government for Mill is, as a result, conditioned by the level of civilization of a people. He establishes no hard and fast rules, or, rather, the rules he sets are second-order rules that could apply at any stage of social development. Governments must promote the virtue and intelligence of their people. These good qualities may then be utilized to carry out the functions of government wisely and justly. In the case of the modern age (his own), he foresees a standard set of governmental responsibilities: law enforcement and jurisprudence, education, finance, and commerce. But it would be fair to say that state action in these spheres is for him best limited. He views education as best provided by private institutions, with any state education existing purely for the purpose of establishing standards and promoting competition.[13] He almost denies that trade and economic matters are his province as a political philosopher, belonging to "political economy," but he suggests that political freedom and free trade have common roots in free individuality.[14] The role of government is to establish broad rules of the game but not to interfere in the economy directly. It may be fair to see this as support for laissez-faire doctrine – minimizing interference in private enterprise – although Mill was enough of a pragmatist to judge each issue on its merits. No statement can express his confidence in the private individual better than this:

> The rights and interests of every … person are only secure from being disregarded when the person interested is himself able, and habitually disposed, to stand up for them … The general prosperity attains a greater height, and is more widely diffused, in proportion to the amount and variety of the personal energies enlisted in promoting it.

But nineteenth century liberalism failed. It failed in one sense because it succumbed to a powerful intellectual critique – to which I shall turn in a moment. It failed historically for a variety of reasons. Its association with laissez-faire economics left it impotent to deal with the political, social, or economic effects of unfortunate economic developments. Moreover, it became associated with the bourgeoisie, whose political vision became clouded and lost focus as the century proceeded and many of whose members abandoned liberalism. It was overshadowed by powerful social and political movements, like the labour movement, and ideologies, like nationalism and socialism, both of which came to exercise a powerful appeal in Western countries.

Yet, liberalism hardly disappeared. It survived as a political tendency within most of our political parties, and indeed, as the core of our political systems. Locke and Mill are part of our everyday heritage, often unconscious, since they have become instinctive. Representative government, the secret ballot, universal suffrage – all themes Mill emphasized – are second nature to us. Enormous attention continues to be focused on civil rights. In our own country, in which there has always been a greater propensity than in our southern neighbour to favour order over freedom, our political, legal, and constitutional system has been transformed by the Canadian Human Rights Act and by the insertion of a Charter of Rights and Freedoms into the Constitution. The man most responsible, one of our staunch advocates of activist government, has equally been one of our staunchest libertarians.[15] On the other hand, although everyone seems to be in favour of freedom, attitudes toward the protection of freedoms and their erosion seem less focused. Few voices are raised when governments invade the liberties of their own people. Freedom has never been more prized, but the dangers to freedom have never been less recognized.

Since language often gets in the way of understanding, let me point out an ambiguity in the use of the term "liberalism." Especially because of usage by our southern neighbour, "liberalism" is now usually defined as the progressive or moderately left-of-centre political tendency. Twentieth century Liberals in Canada practically always see themselves as progressives, not classical liberals. By the same token, old liberals, those whose principles are close to those of Locke or Mill, now tend to be identified as conservatives, because in seeking to defend liberty and fend off the intrusive power of government, many of them are seen to resist "progressive" change. It is, in my view, a serious confusion to identify classical liberalism with conservatism, since the two have very different views on state power. Perhaps the issues will become clearer in the discussion that follows.

There has been no single "critique of liberalism" and I do not propose to single out specific thinkers or political tendencies in what follows. I shall try to convey some representative arguments and positions. Three main lines of attack against liberalism, particularly in the democratic world, have targeted an overemphasis on freedom at the expense of equality, a lack of social and economic sophistication in its central concept of individualism, and a tendency on its part to underestimate the extent of the public or common interest, and in consequence, the legitimate role of government. These have on the whole been launched from a political viewpoint that has dominated our century and resulted in the emergence of highly interventionist government and a vast, universal, social welfare system. In the democratic world, this viewpoint has been seen as compatible with elements of liberalism – civil rights, constitutional government, representative democracy, and so on – but in general political thought in our century has taken us way beyond liberalism in designing the role of government.

The fundamental political principle of our age has been fairness or equality, not freedom. The goal was and is equality of opportunity, so that fundamental rights, benefits, and therefore freedoms can be enjoyed to the maximum by everyone. Liberals, too, believed – believe – in equality of opportunity, but the difference in our century has been the aggressiveness with which governments have sought to achieve equality. Considering that it has a material base, since one's wealth determines to quite an extent one's scope for action, equality of opportunity has tended to merge along its edges with a goal of greater material equality. The two concepts of equality are distinct and the second very much at odds with traditional liberalism.

Not only the Western democratic world has been seized of this principle. Equality has been a principle objective of communism and of the newly independent countries of the Third World by and large. It has been applied internationally, among nations, not just within them, giving rise to anti-imperialism and the vast, if largely ineffective, intergovernmental effort to bring development or shift resources to the Third World in the last four decades. This principle of equality or fairness may be said to be the most important motivating idea of the twentieth century.

Government has been the instrument of choice to tackle inequality and right the balance. However, historically it has not been high principle alone that has led to the erection of the modern Leviathan. Two world wars taught the practitioners of the art of government how to build huge bureaucracies and mobilize practically all the resources of the state for a critical common effort.[16] Military bureaucracies have long provided a model for the rest of government, in retrospect, not at all an apt one much of the time. They were on the whole pioneers in the modern world in the management of large inventories of goods and huge reserves of people. Great social forces in mass society, such as the labour movement, put enormous pressure on governments to bring the benefits of industrial growth to the greatest possible number. But the fundamental vision of equality gave them their legitimacy and motivation to pursue, fight, and win major political battles.

It would be tempting to call this broad tendency and the critique of liberalism that may be associated with it "socialist." However, the marked changes with regard to the role of government in democratic societies in this century have only part of the time, in Canada a small part, been the doing of socialists. It has more often been the political centre that has implemented an anti-liberal agenda. A considerable portion of our intelligentsia, many of our leading writers, some middle-of-the-road politicians, and some of our socialists or social democrats prefer to describe themselves as Tory centralists. Their forebears were responsible for righting the wrong of the American Revolution, as they saw it, by defining the role of government in Canada as "peace, order and good government," with nary a mention of freedom or property. By this emphasis they sought to avoid the consequences of excess of freedom that they claimed to see in the United States, such as unacceptable disorder, even civil war. But in turn they established, or promoted, a political and social tradition of quiescence and subservience to authority in Canada that is quite marked for a democracy.

Tory centralism, with a strong dose of Canadian nationalism, received a powerful intellectual push thirty years ago from an elegant little book, *Lament for a Nation*, by the late George Grant.[17] It poses a powerful argument against the liberalizing influence of the United States (embodied for Grant in the Liberal Party, and more particularly, in its most influential economic leader of the 1940s and 1950s, C.D. Howe) and a defence of conservative values that have come down to us from the Loyalist settlers at the time of the American Revolution. Interventionist government, restrictions on freedom in the public interest, and a degree of anti-capitalism inform the work. It had an enormous impact on a generation of young Canadians – I was certainly one. Among other things it helped give focus to a new generation of confident, skilled Canadian writers from the late 1960s on. The hold of such ideas over Canadian intellectuals has been as remarkable as the attraction of communism to American intellectuals before WWII, or of left-leaning liberalism and later radicalism since the War. *Lament for a Nation* is a striking example of how an idea, simply and persuasively put, can launch a movement and give new life to an older, still powerful political doctrine. But, if my analysis is correct, we should not be too surprised. With all the oddities of Grant's thesis – elitism, questionable arguments against freedom, equally questionable economics, Straussianism,[18] strong affiliations with High Anglicanism – it was a restatement in many respects of the dominant anti-liberal twentieth century tendency.

Socialists of a democratic stripe have had impact up to a point in Canada and elsewhere but we should not overstate their influence. After all, the New Democratic Party and its predecessor, the CCF, have never been in power federally and only sporadically in the provinces. Whatever the extent of the moral authority often claimed for them with regard to public policy, what has become the dominant ideology of government cannot be due only to them.

First, then, traditional liberals are attacked for emphasizing freedom to an extent that is incompatible with equality or, in any case, gives it too little weight. The Achilles heel of Lockean liberalism, according to this view, is its focus on property. Locke wrote in an underdeveloped – not even a developing – country which tolerated enormous disparities in the distribution of wealth. Many consider that he wrote from the standpoint of the propertied classes to whom he belonged, those who had something to lose and were jealous guardians of their wealth. This may or may not have been an assumption of which he was conscious, but it does not matter whether it was or not. What matters is what the theory actually implies or how it was understood by his followers and admirers. Maximize liberty in a society marked by significant inequality and you maximize it first and foremost for those who have the means to exercise it, the wealthy and the privileged. The rich have freedom to do more than the poor. In fact, in Locke's day the poor had little, if any, freedom. They were not like most of our poor, at least in developed countries: they lived amidst such grinding poverty that every ounce of energy was needed for survival. Those better off but without independent means lived in a kind of bondage, dependent on patrons or employers. Thus, Locke's theory of liberty is high-minded in itself but two-faced in practice, once one smokes out its inherent unfairness. Some socialists, particularly Marxists, would say freedom itself is ideology-dependent, in the sense of being in the service of the economically and politically dominant classes who have the privilege of exercising freedom. Most democratic thinkers would not wish to cast doubt upon the very value of freedom; they would insist that freedom must go hand in hand with equality of opportunity, which in turn demands a more equal distribution of wealth.

Was Mill any better, from the point of view of these critics? Well, he was in a way. He was a much more modern man, who defended universal suffrage, from which he excluded neither the propertyless working classes nor women, and freedom of thought, however humble or wrong the purveyor of certain ideas might be. He had a much more lively understanding of equality of opportunity under the law and the importance of universal education. But Mill would not satisfy modern critics of liberalism. Pragmatist though he was, his non-interventionism would not please many in the twentieth century. And, with all the profundity and the idealism of *On Liberty*, and even in light of Mill's active political career as a Victorian reformer, there is something in his eloquent portrayal of intellectual debate that is disembodied, intellectual, the concerns of the book-lined study, distant from social reality.

The role of democratic government, according to the critique, cannot be only to protect the liberty and property of a few. It must have an active role in promoting equality of benefit for all. Its right to tax the property of its citizens on behalf of the greater good, must still, as Locke insisted, be with the consent of the governed, but of all the governed, the rich minority as well as the mass of poor. The role of government must therefore be considerably more invasive than Locke or Mill would have found palatable. Government must redistribute some of the wealth of society even if that reduces the freedom of the rich somewhat, so that the freedom of those who are not rich can be expanded. In Canadian, and most democratic, societies, this has been attempted less through massive socialist intervention in the economy than through the government's financial powers and the social welfare system.

Understandably – to come to the second main criticism of liberalism – Locke was a naive when it came to sociology. Sociology had not been invented yet. Consequently, he thought in terms of individuals and underestimated, passed over too lightly or, perhaps, found to obvious to require discussing, the role, the rights and the power of social groups or classes and organizations. As is often the case in history, the most important factors are those not expressed. The closest he came to showing any understanding of this concept was in his treatment of the extended family, with its male head, its blood relations and its retainers, salaried employees and servants, a now practically extinct social form in the Western world that predominated in pre-modern society.[19] (Small family businesses may still provide a distant analogy, corner stores, for instance.) Society consisted of an aggregation of volcanic mountains of different scales and sizes only the peaks of which, the almost invariably male heads and patrons of each unit, were players in civil society. Moreover, Locke seemed too ready to tolerate the tyrannies within social entities. He made light of the coercive power masters exercised over their servants, children, wives and apprentices, satisfied to state that that power was not absolute since it was impermissible to take life.

More to the point, he took little notice of the evil that privileged classes and organized groups may do in the name of freedom, monopolistic businesses for example, nor of government's role as an arbiter of classes and organizations and protector of individual rights against coercive power exercised by groups other than the state. If society consisted only of landowners, gentlemen farmers, and their extended families, his theories would make more sense. This may explain part of their appeal to the colonial revolutionaries in America, whose society in 1775 was in extraordinarily large measure one of independent farmers. The colonial American preoccupation with checks and balances, in its updated form of liberalism, must be extended – and, indeed, was eventually extended in the United States – beyond government to social groups and organizations at large. An example may be government intervention to protect labour unions and individual industrial workers against their mistreatment by companies and their owners or to ensure fair competition among companies.

There is a more theoretical criticism of Locke from the point of view of social theory, but for those interested, it is worth a paragraph or two. Locke's state of nature is a collation of atomic individuals in competition with one another. Locke seemed to hold that free individuals were primary and society was a construct they, in their wisdom, created.[20] Even Mill, although not without a sense of the historical and social context of liberty, does not seem to grasp the significance of the difference between the liberty and aspirations of a British gentleman and the liberty and aspirations of a Scottish steel worker living in a Glasgow tenement. This, the modern theorist would argue, is a serious falsification of human social reality. Communities, or societies (and their sub-groups), whether classes or not, are in fact primary and make the rules or set the standards in accordance with which individuals must live. Our very language is a social, never an individual, phenomenon. Individuality is a construct that takes its meaning from its social context. That meaning varies from society to society. Individuals do not create society by alienating a part of themselves to a social structure: society and its rules pre-exist. Freedom, accordingly, should not be seen as a primitive possession of individuals or as what they have left after they have assigned some of their liberty to society. It has meaning only in a social context that already constrains them and defines the scope of free action. Maximizing freedom, assuming it is an acceptable principle, can only be done in light of the limitations that prevalent social ideologies place upon individuals.

What would an individual – a free individual – be apart from a society? Can we even imagine such a phenomenon? We can imagine isolation – legendary mountain hunters living on their own, Robinson Crusoe, perhaps – but they are people who have a social context, one that has defined their nature, though they have abandoned it or become cut off from it. Crusoe is an archetypal individual living in a sort of state of nature, but he brings with him all the knowledge and all the assumptions of mercantilist England. The destitute of pre-modern Europe (or for that matter of today) are individuals outside the normal social order, but Locke did not have them specifically in mind. Their individuality was not defined and their wills were not free. In civil war, the existing rules break down and a kind of state of nature rears its head, but anything like a real state of nature, everyone fighting against everyone else, if possible at all, is a momentary phenomenon. A civil war is fought between two well-organized sides with their own principles, objectives, assumptions and social vision, based on their experience as members of society. Superhuman leaders and creators may be as close to the ideal as individuals get, but to the extent they are not creatures of fantasy, they hardly exist outside a social context. They depend on it, manipulate it, dominate it.

Marxism carried this critique to an extreme. Whether or not it is accurate to attribute to Marx a sort of state of nature called "primitive communism," he did in fact believe that the further back one goes in time, the more humanity becomes characterized by collective or communal forms.[21] He refers to humanity's primitive condition as "mere herd-consciousness"; society's goals were all common goals and its members barely existed as conscious individuals. Modern anthropology has been as devastating to such theories as it has to Hobbes and Locke. Both turn out to be highly abstract and remote from empirical reality. Their real purpose seems to be to express the basic moral predilections of the thinker, individuality in the case of Locke, collectivity in the case of Marx. For Marx, rights, liberty and self-realization, when they are legitimate rather than mere bourgeois illusions, are principally collective phenomena; individuals find themselves through the liberation of the working class. Few would accept such a concept as a legitimate form of freedom today, but it has always exercised tremendous influence all around the world, including radicals in the Western world.

Finally, modern critics find ridiculous the exceedingly narrow domain of the common interest as defined by liberal theories. Liberals, they might argue, never arrived at a reasonable understanding of the common interest or of its scope. We therefore find them arguing about the most picayune matters. A British historian writes, "The eighteenth century was the great age of private property ... It is ... to this tender care for rights of property that the refusal of parliament ... to legislate nationally on such matters as the lighting, paving and draining of towns ... must be ascribed. Thus do men's ideals shape the fabric of their environment."[22] Similarly, we in our era of banned substances, find curious Mill's remark that the question of importing opium into China or of selling poisons was essentially one of liberty.[23] On more contemporary issues, intervention by government to deal with the hardships that result from economic development in capitalist societies, a matter with which liberalism never came to grips, is now deemed essential by almost all political tendencies.

What is at issue for us is the extent of such government intervention. At the further left of the scale, some socialists – and some non-socialists – have wished to organize the entire economy as departments of the state and run it through central planning. This notion is largely dead today, but often, quite extensive intervention results from the use of less direct instruments, fiscal power in particular and the universal welfare system. Aside from the issue, exhaustively discussed, of their costs, to what extent are these intrusions necessary or desirable?

Before proceeding to a more thorough analysis of liberalism, let me say a few brief words about liberal movements and liberal thinkers in our century.

The liberal parties that dominated nineteenth century politics have tended to shrink or disappear in this century. Our experience in North America has tended (at least until recently), with some wrinkles, to be toward two-party systems, made up of huge consensus parties occupying the centre of the political turf. In Europe, the liberal parties tended to become representatives of the so-called petit bourgeoisie, the little shopkeepers and white-collar personnel squashed between traditional social forces and big business on the right, and big labour on the left. So desperate did many of these people become that they formed a major constituency of the fascists when they came on the scene. The political history of liberalism in our time has been most inauspicious.

Few in number and on the defensive they may have been but there have been significant liberal thinkers. Recently, liberalism has been making a come-back in intellectual circles in America. I am not at all in a position to be exhaustive but I will mention two main groups.

Earlier in the century a "school" of Austro-Hungarian exiles found its way into the West, starting in the decade after World War I. One of the most important was Joseph Schumpeter, who taught for many years in the United States. The philosopher of science, Sir Karl Popper (1902–94), a resident of England, deserves to be mentioned. His two-volume work, *The Open Society and its Enemies* (1945), although quite rightly not taken seriously as explications of such historical thinkers as Plato and Hegel, is without question a staunch statement of liberal principles. A third, F.A. Hayek (1899–1992), who lived in both England and the United States, has had wide influence in the latter especially. I will have more to say about Hayek, a particularly relevant theorist, in the coming chapter. Links with the past, Popper and Hayek both died in their nineites during this decade, the former only last year. Another "exile," Russian-born Sir Isaiah Berlin, still going in his eighties, was long a confident liberal voice at Oxford, amidst a sea of leftists. His lecture, "Two Concepts of Liberty,"[24] which defends "negative freedom," freedom from interference by others, against the notion of "positive freedom," rational self-realization and its collectivist spinoffs, is a minor classic.

In the case of the United States, we run into vocabulary problems. The outstanding liberal thinker has probably been economist Milton Friedman, but nearly everyone thinks of him as a conservative. Probably he and his thought need to be distinguished from their fans. "Liberal" in the United States, as I have frequently mentioned, tends to mean "progressive," as in "New Deal liberalism." In the last two decades, the phenomenon of "neo-conservatism" has emerged, much of it in the pages of the political and literary journal *Commentary*. An accessible portrait of this phenomenon appears in long-time *Commentary* editor Norman Podhoretz's *Breaking Ranks*.[25] Podhoretz describes his journey from New Deal liberalism to 1960s radicalism, then his break with radicalism in favour of what he calls "centrist liberalism" in the 1970s.

Aside from the singularly American preoccupation of anti-communism, Podhoretz enunciates a number of principles that any liberal would find familiar. He asserts that people's individual desires and ambitions are in themselves natural. It is natural and human to want to be successful, to involve oneself in "the pursuit of happiness," as it is phrased in primordial American thought. It is natural for both individuals and the groups to which they belong to have interests and to pursue those interests. The ideology of disinterestedness, of being above faction and looking at issues from the perspective of the public interest as a whole, as espoused by many American intellectuals, he regards as an illusion. Not only illusory, it proved downright dangerous to democracy in the hands of intolerant radicals in the 1960s. He views equality of opportunity, based on having the same non-discriminatory rules of the game for all, as paramount. He follows this to its logical conclusion and sharply opposes affirmitive action, favouring particular disadvantaged groups, blacks for instance, since he views these as fundamentally discriminatory, even if they are intended to assist them. He supports the free market but also the welfare state as a means of assisting the victims of economic change, but he counsels caution and modesty with regard to tackling huge social and economic problems with governmental instruments. Huge, costly, unrealistic, ambitious failures like Lyndon Johnson's "War on Poverty," for example, taught a generation the limits of governmental power. They raised expectations without delivering the goods: not surprisingly, therefore, their legacy was not sustained social progress but the violent upheavals in the ghettoes in the mid-1960s.

Although I will approach the issues in a different way from Podhoretz, you will see reflections of these positions in the pages to come. Indeed, you will have seen them already in earlier chapters. I will now turn to an analytical re-examination of liberal theory, and in the course of it, will discuss further the critiques of liberalism to which the twentieth century has given rise. My contention will be that there is more that is right in liberal theory and more that is wrong in the interventionist state created by its critics than we have tended to suppose in our century. Liberalism is by far the better bet for the century to come.

CHAPTER NINE

New Liberalism

Freedom of the Individual

For virtually all of us within the democratic spectrum – conservatives, centrists, and social democrats – liberalism is an element that lies at the core of our beliefs. This liberal core has become obscured and distorted in the West during this and the last century by anti-liberal ideologies and the growing power of government. Freedom has increasingly been taken for granted, or treated as of secondary importance and democracy itself has become more vulnerable.

It is important to rehabilitate freedom. This rehabilitation has three facets. First, there is a need to shear the concept of freedom of the negative elements that some of liberalism's critics have uncovered. We have to move beyond the profound and revolutionary, but now archaic liberal theory of John Locke and the pre-twentieth century liberalism of John Stuart Mill. Secondly, a re-examination of the meaning of freedom is required along with a new, or renewed vision of freedom, a renewed sense of its value and its prospects for twenty-first century Canada. Finally, we need to look in more theoretical terms at government and our obligation to government. For the most part, I will save the last subject for the next chapter.

To begin, I suggest we take a walk about the concept of freedom, look it over from all sides and assess where it has come from and where it may be heading. We are concerned with how freedom rates as a human good, at how it relates to other aspects of the moral and political universe, including equality, responsibility, order, and power.

"Freedom" has in these pages two main meanings. In order to rebuild an ideal of freedom we need to examine them both.

"Freedom" is, in the first instance, the power of choice, of being able to do or choose what you want. Crudely, freedom is about maximizing choice without constraint. This is not only a simple view of freedom, it is in a sense childish, fantastic. Only in a dream world can we do everything we want.

However, let us keep our heads clear at the start. Being able to do what you want is not in itself a bad thing. However, it is not always a good thing because other factors may call its goodness into question, but it is in itself quite innocent, as innocent as wanting things that please us.

The second meaning of "freedom" is the notion of independence or autonomy. It is the will and the power to take care of oneself and command one's own life to the greatest extent possible. It is being responsible for oneself. This is so common an idea, being the charge of practically every parent to practically every child, that it has become hackneyed. Yet it is a simple, fundamental moral concept, a core ideal to form character and guide action. It is also a more complex and interesting concept than "freedom" as choice.

Old liberalism belonged to a simpler age. Yet, bearing in mind the formidable critique of the concept – "socialist" arguments and "Canadian" arguments – and all the social change that has occurred, freedom retains its appeal. Liberalism is amazingly resilient.

Its basic tenets are reasonable. Maximizing freedom is a sound principle; freedom is a primary good. I mean by this that maximizing freedom is desirable unless very good reasons are found against it, for example, seeking some greater good or avoiding some dreadful harm. Limiting freedom, on the other hand, is not a primary good. It would not make sense to say that enslavement is good and you need to justify removing shackles. Putting shackles on someone is what needs justifying, not taking them off – unless you are Ivan the Terrible. From a historical perspective, we can see how revolutionary John Locke was in challenging the political wisdom of his day, which proclaimed the divine right of kings to dispose of their subjects more or less as they wished.

To say freedom is a primary good is a way of restating Locke's fundamental principles. It expresses the meaning, or gives a defensible interpretation, of the parable of the state of nature, in which freedom comes first and giving some of it up to the state is secondary. It does not matter that this is not sound history (there was no primitive state of nature in which all humans were free) or sociology (it is true that freedom and individual consciousness emerge only within a social context and do not have much meaning in some societies). It is not supposed to be. It is stating a moral principle, ascribing a value to freedom.

The second Lockean principle, that governmental power should be limited, is a particular case, or logical consequence, of the primacy of freedom. The limitations that law and governmental action place upon the freedom of the individual need to be justified in terms of a greater good, such as a substantial contribution to the public interest or the strengthening of freedom overall. My contention is that freedom has increasingly in our century been taken too lightly in assessing these factors, but they are real factors nonetheless. Conversely, just as restricting freedom is not a primary good, governmental restriction of freedom is never something good for its own sake. They are neither of them primary goods. Despite this, many in government, like the sovereigns of old, view maximizing power, whether deliberately or not at the expense of citizens of the state, as their central objective.

From the moral point of view, some freedoms cannot be taken away ("alienated" was the old word) under any normal circumstances. They are fundamental. You cannot, as crude utilitarianism is supposed to have held, sacrifice one person's liberty arbitrarily in the interest of the liberty or good of the majority, "the greatest good of the greatest number." Moreover, depriving someone of his life, which is his most important possession, is so drastic a step that it is in need of overwhelming justification. Even Hobbes, who saw little scope for freedom in the state, considered the right of flight from a sovereign bent on capital punishment as inalienable. Because of the fundamental nature of the right to preserve one's own life, there is always enormous controversy surrounding "justifiable homicide," capital punishment, even mercy killing.

You will notice that I do not refer to freedom as a "natural right" or an "absolute" good. The notion of natural rights is based on a view of human reason as capable of descrying in nature certain fundamental moral truths. Morality is certainly subject to reasoning and to argument, but its truths do not lie in nature but in our discourse, our frame of reference as human beings. Similarly, the nature of human discourse is such that goods are never absolute. Basic principles are always subject to reflection in the light of new circumstances. We are always having to think them through again. Making a particular good absolute can lead to fanaticism and to the perpetration of startlingly evil acts in the name of good, as when someone espousing the absolute right of a foetus to life tries to kill someone of the opposing view.

Another problem with the term "absolute" is that it is usually contrasted with "relative." "Relative" is a bad, misleading term when it is set up in opposition to "absolute." It is said that if morals are not absolute and unassailable, they must be relative to individuals or societies, subject to choice or preference. This is impoverished thinking. Our basic moral values are shared. They belong to our common discourse. Whether someone should be arbitrarily deprived of his or her freedom is not "relative" to someone's or some society's preference.[1] Rather, one ought never to deprive someone of freedom arbitrarily. Freedom may be taken away only if there is overwhelming justification (the safety of society from a murderer, for example).

How does freedom relate to equality? Is equality a primary good like freedom? These are difficult questions, not only because few will agree on the answers but because they have an inherent complexity. Let us try to sort out some of the confusion.

"Equality," like "freedom," is an ambiguous concept. "Equality" may be used to mean the same as fairness, treating everyone according to the same principles. It may mean a little more than this, the condition in which, to the greatest extent possible, everyone has the same chances in life. The latter conforms to our traditional notion of equality of opportunity. Or "equality" may mean material equality, a situation in which everyone possesses roughly the same level of wealth or receives roughly the same level of income. Alternatively, "fairness," this may not mean that everyone in society receives the same material rewards, but that everyone receives a reward based on one's usefulness or contribution to society.

There is a further distinction, cutting across these senses of "equality," that may be useful to make at the outset. One may look at them, broadly speaking, from the moral point of view and seek to evaluate each; and one can consider the role of government in bringing about various kinds of equality. Sometimes the moral value of something, and the desirability of government action to attain it will accord with one another but sometimes they may not. I will look at the issue of government action shortly.

Equality in its first sense, and up to a point in its second, can be treated as a primary good. It seems that fairness, being treated according to the same rules, is as important as freedom. How do they relate to each other? Do they conflict? Rules constrain people, of course, and will therefore be at loggerheads with the unrestricted freedom of some. But fair rules of the game are a condition for rational action, including free action. They make it possible for all people to have access to freedom on the same terms or, to put it in terms of equality, for everyone to have a fair and equal chance to be free. The conflict, rationally speaking, can be resolved, just as it is resolved by the primitives in Locke's state of nature.

Equality of opportunity, the fair and equal chance to be free, goes beyond fair rules alone. Nature, if I may use that old-fashioned word, may not endow us with equal resources – talents, prowess, beauty – but, these things aside, each of us should have as fair a chance at success and achievement as our fellows. An important social condition is the absence of artificial class distinctions or constraints on people's efforts to better themselves. When elites, whether traditional aristocracies or ruling groups in modern dictatorships, control societies and economies for their own benefit, they control all the main channels for upward mobility. In modern industrial society, a complex array of social forces – one's wealth, parentage, class, place of origin, accidents of birth and circumstance – gives people very unequal access to opportunities. While it is more or less nonsense to say that nature is unfair, social advantage does seem undesirable and unfair.

Material equality and the related notion of a fair, but unequal, distribution of goods are a much more contentious matter. They may be goods but not unblemished ones, and certainly not primary ones. Almost no one, not even a communist who consigns this sort of equality to the never-never-land of an ideal future condition, thinks absolute material equality would be a good thing. We in the democratic world tend to believe it both a practical impossibility and a moral travesty, because effort should be rewarded and not indolence, and because some skills and activities are more useful to society than others. The case for a relative material equality would run something like this: the closer we all are to one another in wealth, the more equal are our chances in life and the fairer is the distribution of freedom among us.

Many consider it unjust – unfair – that certain activities of very high social worth are rewarded much less than others. Is it "fair" that important scholars make average incomes while sports heroes, or entrepreneurs who ride a boom to great wealth, are multimillionaires? Other people may not view material inequality as a bad thing at all, or they may see it as bad in light of such things as how wealth is obtained, how fair the rules of the game are, how poor those at the low end of the spectrum are, or how great the distance between rich and poor is.

Is there a way of bringing these differences of view together? Is there a formula for the fair distribution of wealth that we can all agree on?

The answer is clearly in the negative. The value we assign to various productive activities is usually determined by our own interests. Doctors tend to think doctors are the most important and deserve the biggest share of the pie, lawyers lawyers, blue-collar workers blue-collar workers, artists artists, engineers engineers, and professors professors. Envy may play a big role in such attitudes, as does competitiveness. Obtaining more wealth for yourself or your group is a common inclination.

On the other hand, many may think that we could surely reach agreement if we took a strictly moral point of view. Well, it is not as sure as all that. When we abstract ourselves from direct personal interest and try to take a moral perspective, we tend still to be limited by the view of society we have from where we sit. Even highly righteous people are not very likely to come up with the same answers concerning the relative utility to society of different functions or how they should be compensated. I tend to think that Mozart got a bad deal, that he should have received greater material rewards than practically all of his contemporaries, including his Emperor. This is, moreover, arguably a moral position. But I doubt very much that everyone would agree or that, had I the greatest persuasive and analytical skill in the world, I could persuade everyone of my viewpoint. We who are members of the same society differ too much from one another on moral matters. We differ partly because of personal differences and partly because we come from different social, religious, and ethnic backgrounds. We usually call a society like ours "pluralist" for this reason. However much we share a common background, we cannot harmonize a rationally-based preference simply by an appeal to moral principle. Thus, our views may be moral but still differ. Tolerance becomes a primary virtue in a pluralist society. We differ but live in peace with one another.

But what about the simpler position: the more equally wealth is shared, the more freedom there will be – up to a point, at any rate. People with more means can satisfy more of their desires; they have a greater power of choice. Would it be better if wealth were more equally shared in order to equalize freedom to a greater extent? Some writers reject this notion of freedom, saying it is really power.[2] Freedom is the absence of constraint. However, I have been using "freedom" in the crude sense of maximization of choice, so let us consider it.

A preliminary argument against this notion is that equalizing wealth may not increase wealth. If there is inequality but all or most groups in society are improving their positions, does this not mean that freedom is as a whole increasing? Free marketers certainly believe so. For example, Drucker, quoting Pareto's Law, argues that governments have done almost nothing to bring about greater equality.[3] Instead, equality has tended to vary with productivity, inequalities narrowing in prosperity and widening in recession.[4]

A more general argument is that there is no way to measure and compare the "quantities" of freedom and equality. A "pragmatist's" argument in favour of one or another measure to equalize wealth, and therefore freedom, may seem plausible when taken piecemeal, but how does he or she know where to stop in the absence of agreed means to measure or to count? If freedom is maximization of choice, we do not have yardsticks to measure the extent of freedom except very roughly. Nor can we count up the number of choices people have under the circumstances of different levels of wealth.

If we view freedom and material equality as the opposite poles of a spectrum, it is easy to see that the extremes are unappealing – in fact, dreadful. Absolute equality without freedom is typified by communism, with its massive and intrusive use of state power to enforce a wretched uniformity from which only a tiny elite are exempt. Unbridled freedom without equality might give us a society of wide variations in freedom between a few powerful people – perhaps even one person – at the top and everyone else held in a state of subjection or even slavery. Such a society would hardly be free just because a tiny number of powerful people have the freedom to do almost anything they want. In fact, such a society would be in conflict with our basic belief in fair rules applying equally to everyone.

But if it is easy enough to reject the extremes, is it possible to agree on criteria that would establish a reasonable balance between freedom and equality in between? How much material equality should there be to guarantee a relatively equal or a "fair" distribution of freedom? As already said, there is no mechanical or mathematical means to determine it. We cannot divide freedom and equality in half and come up with a happy medium. Except near the extremes, we cannot assume a continuum in which the more freedom there is, the less equality or vice-versa. We can only make approximate judgments. Different people will come up with different conclusions, even different moral positions.

In its first sense of fairness, playing by the same rules, the governmental role in ensuring equality is not merely justifiable but essential. It is one of its primary roles to establish these basic rules. The legal system, the system of justice, the rule of law, the protection of basic rights, protection against discrimination: these represent precisely the framework that achieves this. Justice must apply without discrimination to everyone. The laws must be written down, stable and published, so that everyone has a fair chance to know what they are and gear his or her actions accordingly. If the rules of the game keep changing, as currently keeps happening – or threatening – in the case of the taxation system, we are always off balance and can never count on being able to enjoy the fruits of our own decisions.

Having the right rules may not be enough. There may be a need for some additional government action to ensure fair and equal treatment for all members of society under the law. This concept is as old as the law itself, but its realization is quite a recent phenomenon and only partial at that. The disadvantaged do not in practice enjoy the legal rights of those with greater resources even today. The rich can always hire better lawyers. The poor often cannot afford lawyers at all. Public defenders, legal aid, a proper education for the officials of our judicial system, recruitment for the judiciary from all social groups and such mechanisms are useful in righting the balance. They are, however, limited and must remain limited, because one could not restructure all society so that everyone has exactly the same position in relation to the law without doing greater damage than these inequalities do, in effect without undermining freedom altogether.

Aside from the rule of law, what about the legitimacy of government action to establish equality of opportunity? The removal of artificial, systemic social constraints may or may not happen through government action, or government action may be only a part, a small part, of the process. For example, the change from traditional society, with its hereditary class distinctions, to modern society evolved through social and economic competition, the free market, with a minimum of direct government action until the process was virtually complete in some countries – Britain is the most obvious case – whereas it was imposed, by revolution or legislation, in some others – revolutionary France and Russia, Austria after World War I, and so on. Government action is justified to ensure laws do not favour rank or station, but more than this is neither necessary nor justified. Even the privileged should have the same rights under the law as everyone else. This problem is hardly relevant to Canada, however, so let us leave the matter at that.

A word is in order here about the notion of "affirmitive action" or quota systems. This is the idea that disadvantaged groups that are underrepresented in institutions or elites (women, visible minorities, homosexuals, the disabled) should receive a helping hand to increase their representation. The merit principle of fair and open competition is to this extent set aside in the interest of a greater good, or righting a greater wrong. Some may argue that this is merely a transitional measure that will fade away once the disadvantaged group is able to compete on its own. Often seen as progressive measures, "positive discrimination" and quota systems are fundamentally flawed. They are indeed discriminatory, since they promote people on the basis of the very characteristics (colour, sex, etc.) fair rules of the game seek to eliminate. Far from being temporary, they may turn into entitlements that are very hard to take away, whether or not the disadvantaged group ceases to be disadvantaged. And, far from being a minor wrinkle in the application of the merit principle or systems of fair competition, such measures are totally at odds with them. They subvert equality of opportunity and increase the scope for arbitrary or less predictable decisions. They confuse or render meaningless what is meant by "fair" and they change the very nature and purpose of the game being played.

Through employment equity legislation and other anti-discriminatory measures, our governments have gone as far as to identify disadvantaged groups and try to ensure against discriminatory treatment of them in fair competitions. Special measures may be required to minimize the effect of built-in prejudices against these groups. But the merit principle and the principle of fair competition are supposed to remain intact. To this extent, governments in Canada have embraced the traditional principle of equality of opportunity and opposed affirmative action. However, practice is another matter. Predilection to discriminate in favour of members of disadvantaged groups is often strong, out of fear of being branded as unprogressive, discriminatory, racist, or conservative. I believe such things happen in the Public Service and in other institutions, like universities – certainly racial quota systems have been well known and continue to be in wide use in American universities, where they are now very difficult to excise despite their increasingly dubious benefits for blacks and for society as a whole. Moreover, tribunals that judge cases of alleged discrimination may be very susceptible to the same sorts of pressures. Charging someone with racism is often an effective terror weapon, no matter how unjust the charge. The political push from activist groups for quotas is still potent but it is also illiberal. It should be resisted.

"Political correctness" is in a sense the height of this perversion of fair rule-systems. The discrimination that is its target is indeed wrong and hateful, but the trouble is that emotion and zeal may undermine clear criteria for when we have broken the rules. Can the analytical study of some religious persuasion be carried out without insulting someone? As the critics of the Rae government's guidelines for university teachers have argued, their effect may be excessive caution, covering up facts or restraining free thought so as to avoid giving offense to some group. Or some faction may interpret the rules any way it wants, as means-justify-the-ends revolutionaries do, turning the matter into a power game. David Mamet's play *Oleanna* is an instructive elaboration of this theme.

The most important social mechanism to make equality of opportunity universal has been education. With the progressive decline of economic obstacles to a full education, more and more people have been able to use their natural talents and knowledge to obtain access to a freer life, a life in which they have more real choices. We can see this happening internationally in the Confucian cultures of East Asia, with their centuries-old tendency to prize education. Society as a whole has a responsibility to afford reasonable access to education to all of its people. Nothing said in Chapter Six, which is about diversifying delivery mechanisms, denies that it is a public responsibility to set standards and ensure access to education for all.

But how much more should government do to equalize the social playing field, given the pervasiveness of social advantage? Just as important, how much more can government do, given the extraordinary intractability of social problems? At the very least, there is a practical constraint. Government should keep to a minimum intervention in social issues that it stands very little chance of being able to influence for the better. Government should by all means react to some social change by assisting its victims, but it has little or no role in trying to guide social change, because neither it nor any other institution can do it, and because the power it would need in order to control social forces would be much more dangerous than the disease. Anyway, as the history of rigidly controlled societies proves, uncontrolled and unpredicted social change, some of it insidious, would still go on.

Should society – or, in effect, government as the chief power in society – take additional action to equalize wealth to a greater degree or distribute it "fairly" as a means of equalizing the freedom greater wealth brings? A few pages ago, I argued that no agreed principles and no measurements existed that could accomplish either goal. It goes without saying, therefore, that no one and no power in society, no experts and no government or governmental organization, can establish such a case. All that a governmental body can do, whether democratic choice is involved or not, is arrive at a distribution that many, even a majority, in society will disagree with. The decision then has to be imposed on large numbers of people. Governments must bring their immense power into play, and once they do this, they may as easily enforce a very wrong distribution. Or they may be susceptible to the influence of some groups in society more than others, giving prominence to a power equation in society that disregards fairness altogether.

Even if their action concerned moral positions on which there is general agreement, governments should rarely use power and coercion to enforce them. The moral sphere, except where action is not just immoral but criminal, should be left to individuals. Indeed, if people are made to do the moral thing, their action ceases to be moral and becomes a mere matter of conformity with law or with power. The implications of this for human responsibility, our responsibility to do the right thing freely and without compulsion, would be immense. When Mill said that governments should not make people do things even if it is for their own good, he enunciated precisely this principle. There will be further discussion of such efforts by government – Prohibition and discouraging smoking are two – in the next chapter.

The following is not too strong a way to put the matter: the case for governments to establish a fair distribution of wealth in society is totally without foundation. Yet, our governments do not seem to think so. The Clerk of the Privy Council has said, as I noted some time ago, that a primary objective of reinvented government is "the creation and fair distribution of wealth."[5] The tax system and the universal welfare system take more, not just in absolute terms but proportionately, from people with more income. Nearly everyone accepts progressive income tax, but that very acceptance is evidence of the hold the doctrine has over us. If it is justified, we need to base it – I hope it is based – on something more than the belief that having more wealth than someone else is unfair. Do we any longer know what these reasons are? Countless statements by politicians, or views in the media that politicians feel bound to "take seriously," seem to assume, willy-nilly, that the middle class or the upper-middle class are fair game simply because they have more than others. Of course, politicians may not really believe this, but they often use it as a pretext to grab resources.

The classic arguments against government action to distribute wealth fairly, arguments that I have mirrored above, were put most succinctly in this century by F.A. Hayek in *The Road to Serfdom*.[6] Hayek's bogey was full socialist planning, which we have noted has been abandoned in democratic countries and increasingly in most others. Nevertheless, his arguments are still relevant since it is the tools used by governments that have changed, not always the objective. Government officials fiddling with the tax rules or enforcing common standards, not minimum standards, of social service may not seem as ignominious to us as economic planning committees, but we need to bear in mind the titanic hold over the economy and society that tax collectors have when they lay claim to some 40 per cent of the national income. Hayek added the controversial argument that such planning was likely to lead to, or prepare the way for, totalitarianism. To capture the full texture of his argument you need to read it. I am content to assert with Hayek that government action to distribute wealth "fairly" is arbitrary (because there is no sound moral or rational foundation for such a distribution of wealth, and because, in consequence, governments are in no position to decide such things better than anyone else), dangerous (because it can only be implemented through coercion and puts power into government hands that can be badly misused), and meddling (because it interferes with actions people can, indeed should, do better on their own). The enforcement of a measure of income equality, or of income levels seen to be fair, limits our freedom well beyond any degree we should accept.

What then is government's legitimate role in redistributing wealth? Or does it have one? It does indeed. Its role is to ensure a minimum standard of living for its people through the welfare system, to keep them above the poverty line, to care for the needy and for victims of economic and social change. This is an aim societies as wealthy as ours should adopt, and relatively speaking, can achieve. All the rest should be left to the free market. Market forces are blind and they may not produce results that our moral selves consider appropriate. We are free to have moral views and act on them – by refusing to pay for the athletic performances that fatten paycheques of those whose sole merit is physical prowess, for example. But no one and no group in society can distribute wealth better or more fairly than the market. Interference in the market only skews the distribution of resources in favour of some group or other. Only the market is conducive to the diffusion of power, the solidity of economic development and the rights of individuals.

In its first sense, absolute freedom would be unrestricted choice. None of us can have unrestricted choice because all sorts of factors, already discussed, always block us. That is a "childish" concept of freedom, the view we hear expressed in the ditty, "I can do anything I want." John Locke and

Thomas Hobbes understood this point perfectly well. The state of nature may start with the fantasy of infinite choice, but it is soon tempered by reality. If two people want the same thing, human reason is called in to work out a *modus vivendi.* The id must be tempered by the ego.

Self-limitation brings us close to the notion of "freedom" as responsibility. A synonym is "independence," as when a young person breaks free from parental control and takes responsibility for his or her own life. The capacity of taking responsibility for oneself to the fullest possible extent is a central ideal of liberalism. Freedom in the simple or childish mode does in a way immediately involve us in responsibility. Acting freely, we may act rightly or wrongly, responsibly or irresponsibly, but we are always held responsible, morally speaking, for our free acts. In that respect, freedom always implies responsibility.

Sometimes the ideal of independence or responsibility has been turned into an entrepreneurial stereotype, like the capitalist myth of Horatio Alger, and other tales that promote the virtues of businessmen and shopkeepers. Such virtues have their point in the context of affairs. The ability to assume responsibility for an enterprise and for the risks one must take to advance it is admirable; it is a sub-set of freedom understood as responsibility. But, like many other value systems transplanted beyond their sphere, it becomes one-sided and ridiculous when applied to life as a whole. We have all known, and probably worked for, small-time entrepreneurs who are unable to understand any value system except their own, unable to respect anyone who is not their own kind. Exploitation in such environments is frequent. I am interested in the more human phenomenon in which we all share, the power to determine our own lives as much as possible and be held accountable for it in the moral sense. In fact, none of us can afford not to take our lives in our own hands. No one is better qualified than we are to exercise power and make choices on our own behalf, not because there is no one smarter than we and no one who can perceive our real interests better – astute observers and professional experts like psychiatrists often do – but because no one can see those interests from our viewpoint better than we can, and because, in the last resort, we are the ones who must act.[7] Being led through a movement like a marionette is not human action.

As in the case of freedom as the power of choice, there is a material dimension to freedom as responsibility. It takes material resources to be independent. We are nearly all dependants of one kind or another. The vast majority, the blue-collar and most white-collar workers, service personnel, sales personnel, have very limited means of governing their own lives, during or even after working hours. Even the highly educated spend most of their lives doing the will of others, some of them ending up with as little time for private life as almost any exploited labourer once had. The vast army of Public Service officials working in the stacked boxes of the bureaucracy following the orders of superiors, provides a pertinent example.

Our culture, our "class consciousness," limits us further. The industrial labourer and some white collar workers too, far from the entrepreneurial ideals of individualism, are often viewed as natural "collectivists," for whom the values of the group are more important than their own. The picket line provides an illustration of how far such "collectivism" may go. The rights and the privacy of members – and even of non-members – of the group are trampled on in the interest of the overriding good of the whole. If this characterization is true, taking responsibility for themselves occupies a lower rung on their moral agenda than group values. Even if one is not a collectivist, one's place on the economic ladder, the material resources at one's disposal, one's education, and one's foresight affect very seriously one's ability to achieve meaningful personal goals.

The twentieth century welfare state has by and large made matters worse, encouraging dependence and passivity. It can be argued – and I agree – that some measures can be liberating, medical insurance the best instance. But the general drift of welfare state policy has been the opposite. There is no earthly reason why the state should impose a retirement income program like the Canada Pension Plan when most people are perfectly able to take care of such matters. Social assistance, too, even medicare, has erred in turning people into dependencies of government and in encouraging the "free lunch" mentality. There are many victims in society in need of assistance, but how many others would be able to take care of themselves if the means and incentives were in existence to encourage them? And how many "con" artists are there who find it easier to live off the welfare system than to earn income for themselves? Even if the percentage is small, the cost to the taxpayer of maintaining these people is high and unjustifiable.[8]

Most people are capable of taking responsibility for themselves and a large proportion of them actively want to do so. Many obstacles can be removed. Conditions that respect the freedom of the individual can be established. As welfare reform envisages, incentives can be built into the system and cheaters eliminated, or some of them. Meanwhile, the right of the vast majority to consume, invest, and enjoy their income should be respected. Part of the plan for reducing government spending must also be a significant reduction in taxes. If people choose to waste their resources, that is their right. Being responsible implies the possibility of being irresponsible. If they prefer collective to individual values, that is also their right. These are part of the moral sphere. But no one has the right or the legitimate expectation to be taken care of when they are quite capable of caring for themselves.

People should take care of themselves, and institutions that discourage them or interfere with them (like our welfare state) are wrong to do so. The trends in the twentieth century have run counter to this ideal, but some of them are beginning to change. Let us look at some examples.

Has liberty progressed or declined in post-war Canada? This is a difficult matter to assess. Material progress has with little doubt been on the plus side. As things went during the Great Depression, an ordinary wage-earner, at least a lucky one who had a job, might make $20 per week; this gave him few choices. He could change jobs at great risk, live in small, rented accommodation, gradually buy basic goods to ensure a reasonable level of comfort, insure himself for about twice his annual salary, and enjoy a good deal of popular entertainment in his leisure hours. Beyond these, it was as well not to be demanding. The choices now for most people are vastly greater and much more affordable.

Have people become less ignorant? The spread of education, especially the opening of post-secondary education to millions for whom the opportunities did not exist a generation ago, suggests that knowledge has increased, so this probably belongs on the plus side as well, despite the serious shortcomings of our public education system.

At least two things stand on the "loss" side of the ledger. The most important one is the huge growth in the power of government, about which enough has been said. With the exceptions noted, government programmes remove more liberty than they provide. More decisions should be left up to individuals, though the passivity of Canadians in standing up for this principle is disconcerting.

The other point, perhaps less prominent in our minds, has been the influence of television and other mid-twentieth century media technologies. Despite the increases in choice as a result of satellites and cable systems, television is and remains an instrument that promotes a near lethal passivity. It is only minimally in our control, non-participatory, a narcotic influence on the young. Such technology, although increasing pleasure and convenience, has been indifferent to freedom or inimical to it. The "choices" it provides are illusory. The high-tech entertainment industries are Big Business, vast, powerful, massively wealthy conglomerates, few in number, that manipulate or ignore the real interests of their huge clientele. The scramble for audience – to give people what they want – produces ever more ingenious spectacles and attractions, the main effect of which is the massaging and the degrading of consciousness, the freedom of choice of the opium den, or, to borrow from Marx, the new opiate of the masses.

So the balance sheet on freedom in the late twentieth century is at best mixed. But there are hopeful signs as well. They reinforce the impetus for a major overhaul in political philosophy and political direction.

Civil libertarianism is at high tide. My generation and later ones have been much more jealous of their rights than any in recent history. The legal profession has developed itself into a powerful instrument to defend and expand rights. The more radical civil liberties outfits are active and influential. The media focus heavily on instances of abuse, or alleged abuse, of rights. Constitutional guarantees have been strengthened. Women's rights, children's rights, native rights, and active discrimination against homosexuals are issues at centre stage. Not all these struggles have been won but the progress in them has been substantial. Nor has every development been positive: the sense that we have "gone too far" in some instances is widespread. Nevertheless, vigilance over our rights is enormously greater than half a century ago.

Children have grown up in the last decades in increasing comfort and protection, and this has spawned new generations insistent on their prerogatives. This is not altogether reassuring: it rests on a kind of self-indulgence and presumptiveness that we as parents and affluent society have willy-nilly encouraged in our young people by being such excellent providers. Less oppressed by poverty or external pressures and able to an extraordinary degree to do what they want, they lack stimulus, incentive, or the sense of need that my generation, and even more, my parents' generation experienced. They are free but not responsible. But this said, they do grow up; they draw large boundaries around themselves within which intrusive powers are not welcome. They will not give up their rights or their freedoms readily.

Consumerism has greatly increased the demands of people for high quality products and services. Industry, in turn, has become increasingly proficient at meeting the demand. Competitiveness – and therefore choice – and quality have never been greater, as firms compete for the dollars of an ageing population. Even the service sector has improved dramatically, partly because of consumer demands and partly because of the central role knowledge (by and large the service industry sells expertise, not products) has come to occupy in the marketplace. The growth of consumerism has helped paint government into the corner it is in, since government has lagged so far behind the private sector in providing quality services.

The decline of the traditional blue-collar working class and the corresponding rise of knowledge workers, whatever the colour of their collars, has been our era's most remarkable social change. The "collectivist" tendency has been diluted as better education, more responsible work, and higher incomes, have made more and more people "middle class." If a large middle class is a fundamental condition of democracy, as de Tocqueville wrote 160 years ago, these changes militate in favour of freedom and democracy.

Information technology is about to open a new era of freedom for us, going well beyond the "choices" that cable systems and pay-TV of the last decade or two have offered us. It will bring to the average home major sources of knowledge and opportunities for interactive communication that will transform both work and leisure. Technology will become an incentive to activity, to thinking, to creativity, not merely a source of torpid, dull pleasure as it has been since at least the inauguration of the TV age.

We should not exaggerate this. Technology, the information superhighway, will offer us an opportunity; it will not guarantee that we will use the opportunity. Titillation is a powerful instrument for the subversion of the will, and masses of people will remain in its thrall. However, the choice will be there, a much more meaningful one than the choice between different channels – candies and their wrappers. A generation raised on video games is attuned to interactive technology and some of its members will see its advantages and exploit them.

Central to liberty has been freedom of expression, but great and indispensable as this has been, the media that control the channels through which views and ideas can be expressed have always been limited. Writing and the print media remain controlled by, relatively speaking, a handful of publishers, who themselves face the inexorable laws of a particularly harsh market. The electronic and telecommunications media are in a still smaller number of hands. However, the essence of "publication" is now changing radically. Everyone who is on the Internet is, or one day will be, able to publish his or her views, work of art, study or treatise. This may produce an explosion of mere volume, but with it there will be a more diverse pool and from it the promise of higher quality. The prospects are bound to be exciting.

Changes in the way business is done, the greater scope for personal responsibility, "empowerment," are also helping alter values in a liberal direction. The breaking down of rigid box-structures and hierarchy in many businesses and the devolution of decision-making downward to the worker are, it seems to me, persistent trends and are likely to be an enduring one. When management guru Tom Peters talks about "everyone an entrepreneur," he is indulging in the outrageous, the hyperbolic, but, however unlikely the vision, it has a core of reality. Peters sees where new values and new technology can lead us: toward much greater independence of action, responsibility and creativity in the workforce. Phenomena like telework and the home-based consultant are driving us toward new, more flexible structures of work that give much more power to the individual. Who would not prefer this to the Kafkaesque world of bureaucracy in which I have spent my career, to the petty exercise of power over others, to systems that degrade rather than improve or encourage?

CHAPTER TEN

NEW LIBERALISM

LIMITING GOVERNMENT

Liberalism means putting the rights and freedoms of individuals first, and delegating powers to government only when necessary. Maximizing freedom of choice and the autonomy of each member of society is primary. Governmental power may be used to create the framework of rules for the freedom of individuals, to defend their freedom or even to increase it in appropriate ways, but liberalism usually counsels protecting liberty by limiting the powers of government. It argues that we should do so not only for pragmatic reasons, such as government's cost, but because it is right to do so: our primary objective ought to be to protect and enhance the freedom and independence of people.

Bad thinking has abetted bad practice. We have too large, powerful, and expensive a structure of government in large part because of a wrong or unbalanced political philosophy. We have overemphasized public action and public power and neglected the creativity of free and responsible citizens. The reverse is also true: bad practice reinforced and actually led to wrong thought. Many individually small pragmatic steps or decisions cumulatively produced a qualitative change in the meaning and concept of government. I have no doubt that a great many thoughtful people consider things advocated in this book to verge on the ridiculous because they find it unimaginable that we should or could undo the knot in which we are now tied. But that was often said about privatization before it proved feasible and effective. We must avoid the trap of thinking that what is, is right. We need to take the longer view. We need to be more aware of alternatives.

So let us complete our walk around the concept of freedom with an examination of its relation to concepts more exclusively from the political or public realm. How does freedom relate to order and power? What obligation do free people owe to government? How in the end can we put government in its place?

Disputes between centre and right often revolve around the opposition of freedom and order. I recall an American correspondent writing some years ago about his inner struggles on becoming a resident of Canada. He could not but applaud the relative cleanliness of Canadian cities, the absence of graffiti from subway walls and the safe streets. But he sensed behind this relative order a difference between Canadians and Americans in the value set upon freedom. If you value freedom more, as Americans tend to, you tolerate more of the mess it may produce. This insight is commonplace. Commentators often refer – as I have done in Chapter Eight – to the contrast between the fundamental principles of "life, liberty and the pursuit of happiness" in the Declaration of Independence and "peace, order and good government," without even mention of freedom, in the British North America Act. The line between freedom and order is drawn in different places in Canada and in the United States. This is a feature of the social and cultural landscape that helps distinguish our two societies. Still, we must examine our attitude as rationally as we can; we should not accept too much order just to be different, if it is incompatible with more important values.

Attachment to "law and order" is often viewed as a conservative principle, but it lies at the heart of liberalism, and indeed, at the heart of all democratic theory. The first justifiable restrictions on freedom that we encounter, according to classic liberalism, rest upon the need to control freedom's excesses, so that the free acts of some do not lead to serious injury to others and the loss of their freedom. Criminal law, the police, the courts, and the prison system are all visible manifestations of this principle. How much order do we need? Liberalism might put this the other way around: how much freedom can we protect?

A fundamental limitation liberalism imposes, therefore, is that everyone in society, the governing as well as the governed, are subject to the same laws. This, once more, is the principle that lawyers call the rule of law. The border between liberalism and non-liberal theories is drawn here; among others it separates Hobbes and Locke. Hobbes held that rule was arbitrary; a sovereign could do anything he wanted, though it was always right for his subject in turn to do the maximum to preserve his own life. Hobbes defended this on the grounds that such "order" is better than the chaos of the state of nature that it replaces. Viewed in a historical context, his position can be understood – his window into the state of nature was provided by the interregnum of the English Civil War when legitimate authority disintegrated and anarchic forces often held sway – but his perspective is too narrow. Locke quite rightly responded that we can do much better than this. We can hold sovereigns to account and thereby enhance peace, order and freedom.

In the twentieth century, crime has been viewed increasingly from a social perspective. What causes criminal behaviour and how can we minimize it? Seen in this light, questions of law and order have increasingly become social issues, issues of equality of opportunity, of education, of improving the income and living standards of the poor. The left in particular has focused on this aspect. The debate is frequently framed in oversimplified terms, some viewing punishment as the only response to crime, others viewing the law enforcement system as a vast social laboratory for the reform of the disadvantaged. The latter was delightfully satirized in Evelyn Waugh's *Decline and Fall*, when the innocent chaplain provided the convicted psychopathic killer with carpenter's tools so that he could work with his hands, and the prisoner promptly carved him up with them.

Social engineering and social work have produced spectacular failures in our times in their efforts to control crime – and very expensive ones, adding to the debt load of governments – but excessive reliance on punishment is equally expensive and has failed us just as much. Peace- and order-loving Canada, I understand, has one of the highest incarceration rates in the democratic world. Simple law-and-order solutions – keeping people locked up without exception and even bringing back capital punishment as the populist right tends to demand – may be effective, where they are effective at all, in only a few high-profile cases. We are often too unaware of the successes of alternative approaches. For example, praise has been given to Quebec's treatment of young offenders, with its accent on rehabilitation. How can we reduce the burden of social deviance on society? How can we reduce our prison population without adding to the social and economic costs and endangering the freedom of law-abiding people? We remain in our infancy in our efforts to understand and deal with these fundamental issues. It behooves us to be modest in our aspirations and practical in our approach.

"Power tends to corrupt," was the maxim of one of liberalism's renowned nineteenth century theorists, Lord Acton. It is, for liberals, a fundamental principle. The power of government, since it is the one institution in society that has a monopoly on violence and because of its immensity, represents the greatest threat to the freedom of society's members. Liberal theory, therefore, gives much thought to ways to keep this power from doing harm. On the other hand, non-liberals have become so focused on what the power of government can achieve that they have lost sight of the threat it poses. Constitutions, laws, and democratic processes are all fundamental features of political society that place checks on governments' power, and if government does not seem so threatening to us much of the time, it may be because these checks and balances are working tolerably well.

However, people may be victimized by bodies or individuals other than government, like criminals for example. Monopolies in the business world may hold their customers to ransom with high prices and poor service simply because the product or service they provide is unavailable from anyone else.

Companies may exploit their employees by paying them poor wages, making them work long hours and providing poor working conditions. The freedom of blue-collar workers and sales personnel was gravely limited before the days of unions and labour protection legislation, and in some sectors it still is today. Liberalism has therefore also favoured checks and balances among institutions to prevent or limit petty tyrannies. Laws and regulation are needed to ensure fair competition, fair play, and protection for the weak.

In this lies another element of the common good and there is a clear role for public power in promoting it. Government may be too strong, as it is today, but it may also be too weak. It is essential that government be strong and authoritative enough not only to control and punish violence, but also to control and remedy non-violent abuse of power in society. It must retain the strength to enter into the game of social and economic checks and balances, so that it is held in check by other organizations but is also capable of checking them when their power gets out of hand. Curiously, Canada has a poorer record in this area that our southern neighbour, where "trust-busting" has a long history. Ours, for well-known historical reasons, has been much more a country of monopolies, nurtured and supported – sometimes even owned – by government.

Checks and balances among levels of government within a single national entity, may be a potent means of limiting government power. I am speaking, of course, of federalism. Perhaps surprisingly, I have neglected this subject, which is so central to Canadian affairs. But I by no means discount its importance. In a country as overmanaged and over-regulated as Canada has been, federalism has played a key and probably indispensable part in keeping governments honest, dividing political power and providing us with different levers to assert control over government and protect our rights and freedoms. The classic liberal statement of the principles and the value of Canadian federalism remains Pierre Elliot Trudeau's *Federalism and the French-Canadians.*[1] It blew the whistle three decades ago on the dangers to liberty that may flow from collectivist nationalism and interventionist, unitary government. Small wonder that Trudeau still elicits such passionate hostility from believers in these ideologies and that his views have become taboo in certain quarters! Interestingly, the electorate of Quebec heeds him more than most of its political elite; Quebec's voters persist in using federalism to achieve equilibrium among very diverse competing forces and views.

Finally, a word, briefer still, about the increasingly critical international perspective. The immense power of our governments may be limited by law, by internal checks and balances among social forces, and by federalism, but governments outside our own nation constrain them even more. Can we relate this factor to liberalism? Can it serve to limit our governments in the interest of our freedom? Not always. In fact, historically not often. The international scene remains a state of nature, an unstable environment governed by no social contract. Foreign bullies frequently oppress other peoples. Free trade, long a liberal slogan, has tended to serve the strong and competitive and drive the weak to perdition. It is no accident that Britain staunchly promoted free trade during the years of its economic ascendancy in the last century. In Canada, the competition of external forces – private or public – has historically been used as a justification for enlarging governmental power and increasing customs duties as a protection against powerful foreign predators, national or corporate. Protectionism, government promotion and then control of transport industries, communications and culture, the National Energy Policy, to name a few, have been responses to external threats to our nationhood from the dynamism and power of others, especially our southern neighbour.

Yet, the liberal ideal of free trade is experiencing a revival. Although there are still many weak countries in the world, there have never been so many that stand to benefit from a "level playing field" in international trade. Barriers are purely negative; they inhibit competitiveness and creativity and increase the costs of goods and services. Competition from others breaks these barriers down, lowers costs to consumers by allowing them to choose cheaper products made by more efficient producers (the idea of comparative advantage) and forces our producers to grow strong or die. Governments are finding that they must draw back from the marketplace in the interest of seeing strong and competitive enterprises develop. In consequence, freedom stands to prosper. In addition, we stand on the verge of a new kind of internationalism, one in which nation states are less viable and less powerful and the balance of forces is not just national but global. Foreign Affairs Minister Ouellet, in presenting the results of the latest foreign policy review to Parliament, said, "The once clear distinction between national and international is quickly becoming blurred." This is so much the case that globalization is seen by many as the most important factor transforming the way our governments operate.[2] In such a world, the opportunities for individuals and the scope for freedom increase to a degree we are scarcely able to grasp.

So might the opportunities for tyranny. Global corporations – multinationals – are less and less the creatures of national governments but they are no less, and possibly more, out of our control than foreign governments are. There is as yet no effective international structure that can enforce responsible conduct on them or ensure a balance of power among them, as national governments, in the liberal paradigm, seek to do. At present, we face no immediate dilemma. There is a relative balance of forces among global corporations. National governments are weaker, but they deserve to be.

However, coping with huge, wealthy, supranational entities is not something we should ignore. It, as a key part of strengthening the international framework in general, may well be the central political issue of the next century.

Many wise heads have anatomized the concepts of "legitimacy" and political obligation. The literature is thick and the intellectual problems many. The old liberals had answers that retain a certain charm but now seem naive, though they continue to excite new work by political philosophers and theorists.[3] The legitimacy of government and political obligation are deduced by Lockean liberals from a "contract" among the members of society. This contract transfers some of their powers to governmental authorities to serve their wider interest in social peace. Locke argued that, if such an arrangement fails to serve our interests, if, in effect, a government is not responsible to its people and acts contrary to their interests or without their consent, it no longer merits their obedience. The people are justified in overthrowing it.

Since democratic governments are responsible to their people in the very real sense that the electorate can "overthrow" them at the ballot box every four or five years, Locke's dicta do not seem to apply to them. They just apply in those countries where illegitimate regimes, ones not based on consent, remain in power. This is, I believe, true, but not as simple or clear-cut as it may appear at first sight. In a number of ways, democratic governments are not so different from governments of other kinds.

This is in large part because all governments behave in accordance with the law of serving number one; government inevitably develops its own interests that may be at variance with the public interest. The public interest is frequently said, by government officials at least, to be what government, the public institution par excellence, wants or decides. But this is patently not the case at least some of the time; frequently, governments appear to act in disregard of the electorate, without its consent.

Even when they do act with the consent of the electorate, they may act arbitrarily, that is, they may sacrifice the freedom or the good of some of society's members. This occurs when a majority support a policy that is in their interest but injurious, severely injurious, to the interests of some minority. This was what Mill called, in a famous phrase, the tyranny of the majority. It is the reason why many liberals, while almost always believing that democracy is the best form of government, point out that democratic forms alone are insufficient to protect liberty. Iran is an interesting case. It has arguably instituted democratically elected government more thoroughly than almost anywhere in the Islamic world, but at the same time it systematically discriminates against minorities like the Ba'hai and enforces – perhaps less so now than a few years ago – a rigid uniformity of belief and practice on its people.

How could we suggest that our own government acts without our consent? Do we not express our consent by voting for, or against, our governments? Up to a point we do, but it is difficult to demonstrate consent in detail. Because the electorate can usually be shown to be ignorant of some, many, or even all of the decisions of government, the concept of tacit consent was invented to legitimize the decisions of governments. This is fair enough. The ignorance of the electorate in a relatively free and open society cannot be a justification for saying they are not subject to government actions, and still less is it a reason for revolution. A certain degree of elitism is reasonable: specialists in government are bound to know more than many of the people they serve. However, this should not be perverted into an ideology that seeks to justify limiting the freedom, level of public participation and knowledge of the electorate.[4] The best friend of a government seeking to avoid restraints on its actions is the passivity of its citizens. How much (or to what extent) citizens wish to participate in public business, should, on the whole, be set by them, not by their rulers.

The welfare area writ large and law enforcement give us the most striking examples, some of them dwelt on with glee by the media, of the misuse of power in democracies. Cases in which police authorities manufacture or suppress evidence, for example, happen enough to cause concern. Although it is dangerous to use the cinema for evidence, the recent film *In the Name of the Father* offers a disturbing instance. Just as disturbing is the way the powers that be in government bureaucracies rally round to defend their institution when it is under attack for wrongdoing. Number one again! It can be countered that these cases are marginal. This may be true in a sense, since they may not be large in number – in any case, I hope they are not. In another, they are not at all marginal. All governments will act arbitrarily some of the time because they have the power and because their aims and their achievements may be seriously at odds with the aims and objectives of the people they ostensibly exist to serve.

Another example of government acting contrary to consent, one I have emphasized repeatedly, is the power governments have taken upon themselves to tax as oppressively as any unrepresentative government the old liberals knew. To be sure, a few ministerial airplane rides aside, our governments do not squander our monies on personal whims or "grandeur" like Versailles; corruption, when found out, is punished severely, sometimes with dismissal or legal action. But government has willy-nilly adopted an adversarial stance toward its own people in the matter of taxes. It does not govern itself by restraint, still less by the "fairness" that it so frequently talks about, but by opportunism. It does whatever it can get away with, and it gets away with a very great deal.

We are entering very sensitive territory, I know. Do these factors justify revolution or civil disobedience? Some of our fellow citizens think so. The words "tax revolt" are being heard in the land – and even in Parliament. More quietly, many people simply refuse to pay taxes. The Auditor-General's Report on 1993 stated that some $6 billion in income tax had not been paid and $1.5 billion in the GST. Smuggling has increased; cigarettes and liquor are prominent examples, but not the only ones. The case of cigarettes is a telling one. In few other instances can a stronger moral, or public interest, case for punitive taxation be made. Cigarettes injure and kill people, even innocents who have the misfortune to breathe other people's exhaled smoke or the plume from ones that are lit. They cost our health system and our insurance companies vast sums of money. They benefit no one but a handful of farmers and cigarette companies. Yet, when large numbers of people are prepared to risk jail in order to resist governmental norms, government has no choice but to back down. Its power and authority are compromised. In a former day, Prohibition was even more catastrophic. Trying to legislate goodness, government instead spawned a generation of organized crime whose descendants, dealing in much more toxic substances, are still very much with us. "Laws don't make people good," a high school history teacher of mine once inveighed while teaching us about Calvinism. Governments should protect the innocent from the dangers of these substances, but it should not, as Mill suggested over a century ago, try to protect people from themselves.

Rules need to be fairly simple. The structure of law is already so arcane that it takes armies of experts (whom we call lawyers) beavering away in libraries and archives just to interpret it, and frequently they disagree, or they compromise their neutrality in the interests of a client. Rules can reach a point of subtlety or unclarity at which they cease to provide clear direction and only arbitrary decisions can settle an issue. Or a rule or law may cease to be general in form, and instead of being non-discriminatory, favour particular groups or people with particular characteristics, like affirmative action or "positive discrimination," which I have discussed sufficiently in the preceding chapter.

Not only are there limits on the types of laws and rules that can be imposed; it may also be counterproductive to have too many rules, even good rules. These days we are overwhelmed by them. But, despite this, fewer and fewer people seem to be observing them. This is a claim that falls well short of empirical test, I admit. It rests on impressions – of how people behave on the roads, of their reactions to signs (ours is a world of signs), of declining public courtesies, of smokers in no-smoking zones. It seems a tremendous irony that so many people are busy producing so many rules that get ignored. If any of this is right, its explanation may be that excessive regimentation produces the opposite of what it intends, massive rule-breaking and disaffection from rule-directed behaviour. It leads to revolt. This is serious because it means that both good rules and bad get violated without distinction. We probably need to pull back from our Levitical obsession with rules and tolerate more mess. We need, equally, to reconsider which ones are really important and which ones are not. We need to leave more things to individuals to decide. They must take their own risks and pay their own consequences.

Rules and laws are in widespread disrepute, but does this mean we should break them? Is defiance of the law and of public authority right? On the one hand, the rapacity of governments and their love-affair with power are wrong. These are public vices that encourage disrespect for the law. Because government takes what it wants from its people without due restraint, it loses public trust and encourages lawbreaking.

At the same time, lawbreaking can almost never be condoned, and not only because lawbreakers might get caught and punished. It produces more serious harm than the harm it seeks to cure. The overthrow of a democratic government by force would be catastrophic, because the old Churchillian truism *is* true: democracy is a dreadful form of government, but all the others are worse, considerably worse.

What about non-violent defiance of the law? Civil disobedience has a distinguished pedigree. In modern democratic thought, it is identified with the nineteenth century American writer Henry David Thoreau who invented the phrase and once went to jail for refusing to pay his taxes. He considered it his right to secede from society and live in self-supported isolation. His thought has provided an intellectual vehicle for many high-minded factions trying to bring about social or political change, most notably the American civil rights movement, nonviolent anticolonial movements like Ghandi's, and the anti-Vietnam movements of the 1960s and 1970s.

What these examples, or some of them, show is that sometimes civil disobedience is justified. It is justified when it is nonviolent and when conditions comparable to arbitrary or dictatorial rule exist. The disenfranchised, segregated black of the American South was as oppressed and victimized as any subject of a dictatorial or colonial regime. They stood outside the "social contract" and were provided with no legitimate outlet for political action. Breaking laws was the only alternative to quiescence in tyranny.

During the turbulent 1960s, people went much farther. Relatively moderate people said that one should disobey any unjust law. The ground under this is much shakier. For who is to decide what laws are just and what laws are unjust? Is it right for people to disobey any law with which they disagree? Civil disobedience should be reserved for the most blatant and harmful of "unjust laws," like the "laws" and edicts of arbitrary rule, or the deprivation of a group's or a class's fundamental civil rights. If one goes beyond this narrow range of cases, wider disrespect for all laws – anarchy – will result. In most instances we ought to compromise our individuality and abide by laws with which we disagree or which we consider wrong in order to preserve respect for the law in general, while working as actively as we see fit to change them.

If the rapacity of our governments, their eagerness to tax us beyond all measure, is wrong, should we take Thoreau's road and refuse to pay taxes? We cannot take tyranny lightly and we must seek to end it, but we should not take action that would undermine respect for the law, deepen our financial crisis, and cause anarchy. It is better to keep throwing out such governments at the ballot box until they learn their lesson. Thoreau has something to teach our time, but his lessons must be applied with discretion. It is impossible to argue that a person owes no obligation to society, because almost everyone receives benefits from it. Certainly the highly educated and principled Thoreau did.

If, on the other hand, our governments never learn, if they bring us to our knees with their catastrophic fiscal policies, if they victimize increasing numbers and themselves induce political and social anarchy, none of the normal rules will apply and revolutionary liberal thought will come into its own again. We will need a new Hobbes and a new Locke to create a new order.

Liberal theory advocates limiting government in order to enlarge the sphere of freedom of individuals. This is no paradox: it is straightforward and clear. There is, however, a social perspective on this issue, with which I will close.

There is only so much that government is fitted to do. Government has never been an innovator, a producer, an institution for which time is as valued as in the private sector. Great social visions – J.F.K.'s Camelot, Lyndon Johnson's Great Society, Trudeau's Just Society – inspire us, but when we try to achieve them unpredicted and unplanned things begin to happen, the goal itself remaining elusive, and the benefits are mixed. Society has incurred some benefits, but it is doubtful they have outweighed their increasingly catastrophic costs.

As with most absolute statements, exceptions may be found to these, but they are usually ones that prove the rule. Government provides a safety net to some people who would live in desperation without it, and government should do so. Extraordinarily gifted researchers and technicians may work for government agencies and come up with miraculous discoveries and inventions. However, with few exceptions – perhaps the nuclear medicine industry was one – government has neither the knowledge, the motivation, the risk-taking capacity nor the discipline of the bottom line to turn most of these into winners. The norm in government is to do things as they have always been done, to bury them in bureaucracy, to discourage adventure, to be safe and to spend one's budget regardless of whether it is spent well. Courses that are mistaken and products that are useless do not get penalized. After every leap there is always a soft landing. Governments often have the resources to make uneconomic production happen. Such innovation, creativity, and entrepreneurial skill as are to be found – apart from what belongs to gifted individuals – is a mirror of our broader culture, our liberal tradition, which has always, even in decline, promoted individual responsibility and initiative to a certain extent.

The incapacity of government to orchestrate social and economic change is not a mere matter of inefficiency or incompetence. Government's actions, government planning, do have effects, huge ones, but they are often different from the ones that were intended. There are, indeed, two central paradoxes of liberalism at work here: that what we plan often bears little resemblance to what we achieve, and that good intentions – of the best people – frequently produce untoward, even evil, results. Why should this be?

Philosophers might remind us that the object of a desire or intention is nothing real; whether we achieve it depends on numerous real-life conditions that, even in the case of individual action, frequently keep us from grasping it. Social reality cannot be reduced to predictability. I am not advocating radical scepticism about the social sciences by any means. Rather, as almost any practitioner in the field would admit, explanation and prediction in the social and political spheres are problematic. Still less is it possible to invent practical applications of the social sciences that have cut-and-dried, predictable results. Social work and "social engineering" are inexact arts, much more so than engineering based on the physical sciences. Why?

Social reality contains a lot of chaos. People do surprising things because they have a choice concerning what they will do. People invent new things that have effects never before charted. The history of technological innovation very clearly proves this point. In general, there are too many "variables" in the human world, as the economist likes to put it, so that many judgments are probabilities, not certainties. Society will not submit to any mechanical or deductive system. We always need to strive to understand it. I expect we are getting better at it but we must always be realistic about the chances of success.

As a result, we need to be much less sanguine about the prospects of realizing our social goals, about the efficacy of social action. The creativity that makes for social progress resides only marginally in government, if at all. It is out there, in the world of people and the organizations they create.[5] Only some of this "progress" is good. Many developments – "development" is a more neutral word – are harmful or neither good nor bad, or they can be made good for us only by being channelled in particular ways. Sometimes, therefore, they need to be made subject to laws and regulations, we need to assist those affected adversely by them, but most of the time we should leave them alone, accept diversity as natural, tolerate them as the price we pay for the many good things that flow from human ingenuity.

The second paradox is now readily comprehensible but it naturally appears counterintuitive: how can the best people be guilty of bringing about bad consequences? The converse also seems bizarre: how can ill-intentioned or amoral people, out to do no more than make a buck perhaps, produce greater social benefit than good people do?

In fact, the best and many of the brightest people I have ever known, people with the highest moral ideals, people with the greatest compassion for the downtrodden, are believers in interventionist government. Many of them have gone into government services precisely to put their beliefs into practice. Often they came from religious backgrounds. The "social gospel" seemed to them a powerful ideology to bring moral principles to bear on social problems. Or, secular visionaries, they saw social work as the means to bring respite to those who were disadvantaged. They eschewed a hunger for wealth, which they saw as the dominant motive of their peers destined for the business world. They may have been a minority in all spheres of life, including government – I have no way of knowing – but their influence on our institutions and our values has surely been powerful.

Yet, the results of all this goodness are, to say the least, disappointing. How is it that so many ideals have gone awry, that what government ends up as is the blunt instrument described in some detail at the beginning of this essay?

There are many answers one could give and perhaps they all share in the explanation. One might be that idealists come to be co-opted by the system. Entering a world that was humdrum, hierarchical, cautious, self-serving and power-oriented, they soon had little choice but to adopt its values. They too had lives to lead, ambitions to satisfy and families to feed. None of us is uniformly or permanently good. We all have weaknesses and failings and can be tempted by less worthy aims.

Or perhaps they did not get co-opted, but were simply overwhelmed. Having no idea what kind of world they were entering, what bureaucracy really is like, what laws it operates by, they failed to master it and turn it to good purposes. Doing good is, after all, impeded by, if not incompatible with, the nature of government much of the time – power, hierarchy, caution, self-protection, turf. It may be that most of them found it impossible to accept that this should be the case or to cope with the many in government with less pure intentions than theirs. The bad eggs tend to ruin the rest (Hobbes' law). Good people do not drag everyone else up the scale of virtue nearly as much as bad people pull everybody down to their level.

Yet, some good people who are neither co-opted nor overwhelmed still take actions with untoward results even when they are in effective control of the instruments of power. Again, why?

In part, it is because government's mission has been wrongly defined if it is seen as a moral mission. Moral purposes cannot be achieved consistently by governments. Goodness cannot be imposed by instruments that are essentially coercive. As I argued in the last chapter, governments cannot create a fair distribution of wealth, because no human intelligence can decide fairly what such a distribution should be. Such things must be left to the impersonal forces of the market because worse things result when they are not. And morality must be left to free individuals, because only free actors can be moral.

Good people too often assume that other people are more virtuous than they are. Now, some people are better than others. But idealists frequently underestimate the mix of motives that take people into the private sector and the longer-term benefits of their short-term pursuit of profit, or the discipline that profit itself imposes. And they overestimate the capacity of ordinary people for altruism. Many individuals and organizations try to cheat the system (both individuals and corporations, it turns out, abuse UIC); criminals fail to live up to society's effort to "reform" them; the vast majority of tolerably upright people overuse, and even abuse, benefits that cost them nothing. Individual interest is almost always a more powerful force than the common interest. These attitudes shock idealists and make them indignant. What they need is simply greater realism. Goodness may increase – I hope it does – but I doubt very much that we are destined to become dramatically better than we are now or for a long time have been.

Finally, we come back to the simple truth of the first paradox. Between intention and action falls, well, if not the shadow, as T.S. Eliot said, at least many things that will not bend in the direction the human will wants.

Government is hard-pressed just to keep up with social forces and with the consequences of even its own actions. It should let the horses run, focusing on some things that need remedy and setting aside others with which it cannot, and does not need to cope with. Many in politics understand this quite well, but their actions often run counter. When the opposition in Parliament or a reporter puts a difficult question to a minister, the assumption they all seem to share is that, however impossible the task, government ought to be able to handle it and should be blamed if it cannot: social deviance, technological innovation, trade imbalances, cultural survival, national unity, eradicating poverty abroad, the weather. The overriding belief is that government HAS TO DO SOMETHING. Inevitably, it does, and what it does is usually part panic and part hubris. The result may be a "programme" – like subsidies for somebody or other – that is supposed to be a cure-all, but often just complicates the problem and means added cost. Then, such programmes become semi-permanent fixtures, because government is inept when it comes to assessing its priorities and dropping its unessential or misguided tasks. Some constituency will always exist that benefits from them. The vicious circle rolls on.

The belief in the benign and superhuman efficacy of government is not an illusion that will go away easily or of its own accord until grandiosity of aspiration in, and for, government changes. We all need to expect less of government. There needs to be an ethos in government and in society that accepts the fundamental limitations of institutional action.

Of course, government should still try to improve. Less imagination would surely not be advantageous. If government achieved all the efficiencies that Chapter Seven envisages, it would be a better, more responsive mechanism. Changing the rules under which government does its business can eliminate some of the flaws that liberalism diagnoses, as the Australians seem to have done in large part simply by reforming the process of budget-making and budget-management. But in carrying out its goals, government should stay within narrow policy and cost parameters. It should take risks to bring about better service – but not with our money. Venture capitalism belongs in the private sector.

Liberalism can inspire but it is less grandiose and more modest than a more idealistic vision. Unfortunately, the politics that I am recommending is reminiscent of Mackenzie King with his legendary caution and the avuncular Louis St. Laurent, two radically uncharismatic leaders. It is open to question whether either of them could get elected today. Yet, there is inspiration, too, to be found in realism, shaping finite goals, achieving some of them, revising approaches so as to get closer to achieving others, and releasing the vast energies that prosper in the larger world of human endeavour.

There is inspiration in a vision of balance among the institutional forces that shape our lives, and between all these and the sphere of individual freedom. What size of government is best suited to such balance? It would be foolish to set an arbitrary number, but, for a start, it might be worth it to envisage government cut in half. If the absorption of close to 40 per cent of GDP through taxation is ridiculously high, let us set a target of 20 per cent for all levels of government in Canada. Some will laugh at such an idea but we are not so far off. At the federal level, if we eliminate debt service and implement all of the savings identified by Programme Review, we shall nearly halve the size and cost of the central government. In the spirit of open enquiry and empiricism, we should make trial of this and see how it might work.

The public domain will remain. Its importance to us as the repository of what we hold in common and as the instrument for what we wish to do in common seems to me undoubted. However, respect for common institutions is greatest when it is freely given by free individuals acting in their own interest, not when it is coerced out of them by power so awesome that they can neither control it nor dissent.

CHAPTER ELEVEN

JUMPING TO CONCLUSIONS

This essay has been an exploration. It may be fairly described as a collection of studies and observations, running from the nitty-gritty to the abstract. It may even appear to be a disparate one. Even though connections have been made, you may find some of them tenuous. A reader has commented that the whole thing might have been done in reverse, starting from theoretical principles and ending with real-life problems and their possible solutions. But then this would not have been an exploration. In fact, it embodies my own journey from inchoate experience and fulminating dissatisfactions through analysis and study to some conclusions or at least hypotheses. It has been a means of sorting out my own principles and beliefs.

However, the charge of disconnectedness has sufficient merit that I will try to draw out of the foregoing caravan some main conclusions, grand hypotheses, if you will, that I have developed and argued for. These hypotheses may strike you as surprising, even if you have seen them already in the text. They *should* strike you as surprising – as they strike me some of the time! – because they subvert many of the common beliefs we share about our political system and that we see or hear expressed by most people in the know, commentators, politicians and officials. They also take into account a much bigger picture of social reality than we are used to seeing or to being shown.

To arrive at the first of these broad principles or "grand hypotheses," we need to look back at the first three chapters. From a limited perspective, they identify problems which the next four chapters take a shot at analyzing and addressing. This is far-reaching in itself. Whether or not they would be the same in content, no ideas more extensive or more radical are likely to come out of the political apparatus or the bureaucracy than ones with the scope of these. Yet, what I am suggesting is much more radical still.

I am suggesting that the ills of government described earlier – debt, waste, flawed management, poor service – are evidence that the dominant political philosophy of our time, the notion of highly interventionist government, has failed. We have conducted a vast and uncontrolled experiment in politics in our century and it has produced, in many instances, the opposite of what was intended. The debt is equal almost to a whole year's national income, costly management of programmes, performance and expenditure whose value to us is rarely measured and often not measurable, excessive hierarchy and control systems, confusion of purpose, a self-serving ethos in government in the whole and in its parts – these are not little flaws needing band-aids but signs of a vision gone wrong. Our approach to government needs to be rethought from the ground up and from the top down. Patchwork solutions – whether they come from the left or from the right – will do little to tackle the immensity of the calamity we, on the launching pad into the next millennium, now face.

The starting point is an old principle: individuals and their desires and interests are primary. They must be able to pursue them freely, to the maximum that conditions permit. Even this fairly pedestrian principle is controversial. A ton of religious tradition and moral training has tended to make many of us feel guilty about our desires and interests, but they are natural and innocent in themselves and they are always of value to those who are their possessors. It is only when they arbitrarily inhibit or destroy the like desires and interests of other members of society that they are wrong, for then they run contrary to the fundamental moral principle of fairness.

If, this limiting factor aside, our interests as individuals are primary, the principal purpose of society in general and of government in particular is to serve those interests and maximize the freedom we should enjoy to pursue them. If we put this more concretely, we find we have stumbled upon another surprising proposition: a government's fundamental obligation is to leave in individual hands a maximum of resources. The aim of government should be to minimize its own share of the nation's wealth, to be modest and prudent in establishing programmes, to administer them frugally and to keep taxes low. Of course, we all know that its overwhelming tendency is to do the opposite. This is the reality we all accept but why should we? How could we ever have been persuaded of the reasonableness of keeping less and giving governments more?

This is far from the whole story, admittedly. Its surprising quality is due in part to the fact that it is not the whole truth. It sounds like the old saw, that "that government governs best that governs least," but this, whether or not we accept it as true, is wholly negative and not very helpful. It does not give us any guidance as to what things government *should* do, what role it should play, nor does it insist that government do well what it is given to do. After all, some of the things governments do are of value to us and they need sufficient resources to be able to carry them out. So let us back up a little and fill in some important gaps.

The leap we have just taken from individuals to government and the role of government is a great leap. There is a great deal in between, much of it inhibiting the freedom of individuals to pursue their interests as much as or more than governments do. The fact is that few of us get to pursue our interests as freely as we wish. In fact, unless we are very rich, or had the luck to choose careers that are every bit what we would do with our lives if we did not have to earn a salary, we spend the great majority of our time pursuing the interests of others, or interests that are not exclusively ours because we share them with others. Most of us, in our places of work where we spend the greater part of our waking hours, submerge our interests in the goals and interests of some sort of enterprise or institution. Even our off-hours are affected. What Coca-Cola employee would spend his evenings drinking, let alone promoting, Pepsi? For many, this may not be a bad thing. Identification with a larger entity gives people's lives meaning, frees them from the burden of choice which many would be unable to handle, and engenders a degree of social stability. Independence is more an ideal, a liberal ideal, and we need to tailor it to realities. At the same time, some people, the hereditary rich, have always had maximum freedom of choice and there is no reason in principle why those who have less wealth should be less capable of handling it.

Society is not a mere collection of individuals, some of whom may gather more wealth and more power than others, as Hobbes and Locke seem to have thought. It consists also of groups and organizations to which individuals belong, voluntarily (up to a point, to one's company, church or political party, let us say) or involuntarily (to one's ethnic group or, originally anyway, to one's social class). Clearly, organizations pursue interests that are quite separate from the interests of individuals. Just as in the case of individuals, there is nothing wrong or insidious about this. The interests of many groups and organizations come to compete with one another on the larger social canvas, but as long as the same rules of the game apply to every group or organization playing in a particular game, such competition is considered fair. However, unlike the rules that apply to individuals, it is also considered fair if an organization is driven out of existence by such competition. This is a characteristic of the free market. A business that attracts more customers may drive a competitor out of business. Advances in products and better technology do the same. This principle does not apply only in economic affairs. It is a feature of open, pluralistic societies in general, applying to any organization for which there are standards of success and failure, such as churches, advocacy groups, humanitarian societies, political parties.

On the other hand, although organizations may wipe out other organizations and be said to do so fairly, they may not by the same token wipe out individuals. Individuals should not be maimed, terrorized or murdered. Indeed, in more positive terms, they must be left the freedom to pursue their desires and interests, whether in terms of leisure activities, family, property, employment or belief. If they choose no longer to share the objectives of a group or organization to which they voluntarily belong, they must be free to leave. Individuals who injure other individuals are criminals, and so are collectivities that do such things to individuals. But another term that may be introduced to describe oppressive behaviour on the part of a group against an individual is tyranny. In fact, where competition prevails, businesses are likely to treat individuals, *qua* consumers, well or they will go under themselves. The "take it or leave it" brand of customer service is no longer conducive to survival. Private companies and many other organizations are paying very close attention to consumer wishes, a trend that increases the prospects for freedom of choice.

Another consequence of the "open society" is that, when organizations go under, the individuals that are part of them are directly affected. If the organization is a company that goes out of business, "downsizes," or even makes internal changes, people may become unemployed. If some other type of social organization collapses or undergoes a major change, there is often an enormous impact on both society and the individuals who belong to it. Beleaguered groups, including even groups to which we belong involuntarily like ethnic groups, may become dissatisfied and driven to radicalism or crime or terrorism, or perhaps to ennui and demoralization, as occurred to native peoples on this continent.

Society, in short, cannot be fitted into a neat package. Social competition and interaction give rise to problems that complicate the picture the original liberal theorists painted and make them liable to the charges critics directed at them. Individuals and the freedom of individuals are enormously affected by these factors.

Governments may differ from other social organizations in several respects. They differ in breadth of clientele, since their public consists of everyone – individual or collective. Membership in a political entity is voluntary only to the extent that one may leave it and live in another. Governments differ in having relative pre-eminence over everything else. All must obey their laws. Finally, they differ in power, since they have a monopoly on the use of force. But despite all these differences – this is the next of our unsettling hypotheses – government resembles other social organizations qualitatively more than it differs from them. It is another collectivity competing on the social canvas, just bigger than all the rest, and, like all the others, it has and pursues its own interests and ambitions. Because of its size and pre-eminence, it has the capacity to be the biggest tyrant of all.

It is hard, because of linguistic usage, to call its interests private interests. If we do, we get into a big verbal mess. Nevertheless, these ambitions and interests are just like private interests in important respects. They involve pursuing the organization's own advantage regardless of the interests of the public, even though its *raison d'être* is to serve the public interest. When government seeks to maximize its power and its share of society's resources, it is pursuing its own interest much more often than it is pursuing the interest of its people. Although "profit" does not come into it as much as power, it is just like a private corporation in this respect. When, at a lower level, a governmental unit seeks to increase its power and resources, or wastes its budget in the run-up to the fiscal year-end rather than return the surplus to the taxpayers, it is pursuing a yet narrower interest, the interest of a part of the organization, still farther removed from the public interest. I called the principle that explains this "Hobbes' Law," extrapolating it from a "law" Hobbes applied to individuals. In a totalitarian society, these quasi-private interests of government drive out practically all other interests. Everyone is forced to conform with them. In such societies, governments and people end up serving virtually no interests except the interests of the government, but the notion of the public interest then loses all meaning.

Much political thought would not accept this thesis. (Nor will you if by now you are fed up with paradoxes.) We do not usually think in these terms. Rather, we think of governments as existing to serve the common interest, though they may do so well or badly and be held accountable if they fail to do it well. In fact, a tension exists between governments' function of serving the common interest and its propensity, like any other social organization, to seek its own interests. This calls for some remedy. What is the common or the public interest, anyway? Does it really exist? How do we define or determine it? Governments' role is usually considered to be nothing more nor less than pursuing society's "common" aims. Does this have real meaning?

Some thinkers believe, or have believed, that there is a definable common interest that everyone in society shares and they identify it with the proper business of government and even the proper essence of humanity. This was the view of Jean-Jacques Rousseau. A legislature for Rousseau is not just a forum in which competitive interests are represented and in which some prevail over others from time to time. It is the place where, through discussion and debate, Reason determines what the General Will, the interest common to all of us, is. A legislature is a sort of scientific team seeking out the same truths.

However, I would hazard that there is no such thing as a common will discernible by reason. The best we could do would be to extract empirically from individual desires and interests what all have in common but, although some interests may come close, there are no desires and interests absolutely *all* people in society share, probably not even (*pace* Hobbes) the desire for the preservation of our own lives. The common interest is relative and changeable. In eighteenth century England, it did not include sewer construction and maintenance. It is the business of politics, not reason, to determine, from time to time and from year to year, what the dominant common or public interests of society are. The process is more political than rational. Thus, it is the model of competing interests in Parliament or in an open political society as a whole that gives the notion of the common interest reality. These may be thought of as our "baser instincts," but Rousseau's view of the common interest, the General Will, is really much worse, because it is incipiently authoritarian. It leaves the determination of the common interest, in practice, to a central authority, a central authority that, if you have accepted my hypothesis, is not to be trusted no matter how great and wise its members are, because its interests and advantage are really like the interests and advantage of a private organization. Rousseau, and the very great philosopher Immanuel Kant, with whom he seems to have shared a conviction about the importance and the sanctity of moral reason, were extraordinarily high-minded men. But when we see the results of such high-mindedness in real institutions and hard-nosed, competitive politics – the centralism and collectivism of the French Revolution is one telling example – systems of open, competitive formulation of public policy do not look nearly so base.

A more contemporary view is that some people in society are better placed than others to figure out what the common or public interest is, particularly intellectuals. Intellectuals may argue that they are "experts" in the public interest because they do not represent particular interests the way businessmen do and they can look with fair objectivity upon issues. They may also claim to be the most intelligent among us. This sort of assumption has lain behind many progressive and radical movements, including a fair chunk of "liberalism" in the U.S., using the term in the traditional "New Deal" sense it has had there.

Unfortunately, although the independence of intellectuals is highly to be valued and is indispensable to the pursuit of truth and the countering of the illusions to which the interested parties that make up society repeatedly give rise, there is little reason to believe this claim. First, intellectuals tend to disagree with one another about political aims, sometimes carrying their disagreements to extremities. Secondly, it is not at all clear that they are always disinterested. They often speak from particular points of view, whether they arrive at them on their own or inherit them from a group to which they belong. Thirdly, their very rootlessness, their "objectivity," can be a danger; it may lead to ideas that are unrealistic and remote from real life and may thus cause great havoc when they are applied. Fourthly, intellectuals do not seem markedly more tolerant of the opinions of others than anyone else in society. I was always told that education taught us to be tolerant. I continue to believe that it does: knowledge always gives us a wider and fairer purview than ignorance. But we repeatedly witness intellectuals stampeding one another into "correct" positions, as they did in the radical 1960s. Fifthly – and this may help explain the preceding point – when intellectuals step into public life, they operate pretty much like everyone else in the political elites. They do not seem wiser or more adept at determining the public interest, still less at realizing it, than many others are. If they maintain a superior pose, a claim to know better than others, they become incipient totalitarians, as Hayek observed of some of the English intellectual socialists of his day. Intellectuals belong in politics like anyone else who is interested, and their comments are most likely to enrich debate, but they have no special status. There is no substitute for the competitive game of politics in determining the public interest.

Without belabouring the issues fairly exhaustively discussed already in Chapters Four to Six, I would like to draw attention to them briefly, since they offer a picture of the "common interest," the legitimate role of government, pared back to a minimum that is affordable and in keeping with a liberal approach.

The elements include, first, establishing the most basic rules of the social game by which both individuals and groups and organizations must abide in their best interest: constitutions, the protection of human rights, the rules of competition among organizations, like corporations, protection for the employed, like the freedom of labour to organize. A lot of regulatory activity may belong in this category, since it establishes basic rules about safety, the environment, and other such things on which our interests as individuals depend.

Secondly, governments must ensure that these rules apply to all persons alike and without discrimination. This is the primary way governments have of defending and promoting equality of opportunity, so that the chances of success may be based on merit alone. A more active form of intervention is the provision of universal education, but this essay's advice is that we should be very wary of ambitious social programmes designed to reduce inequalities, not because there is anything good about these inequalities, but because mechanisms to tackle them are so often costly and intrusive failures that skew market forces and leave even greater unfairness in their wake.

Thirdly, governments must take care of the victims of social and economic change by assisting affected individuals – through welfare, for example. We have seen that individuals may suffer excessively from the actions of organizations in society. Governments are not capable of guiding social change in such a way as to eliminate these impacts, and it is critical to the survival of human freedom that they not try except in very modest ways. Huge social programmes with grandiose objectives, like the American "War on Poverty," are beyond the power of governments and should be avoided. Nevertheless, it is morally unacceptable to abandon society's victims. We may – indeed we ought to be able to – find much more effective ways of using the welfare instrument to rehabilitate people, but this does not call into question the need for the instrument itself or its moral necessity. I fear that much of the orneriness we now hear about welfare and about those on welfare expresses the opposite point of view, a wish to abandon victims and a denial of society's obligations toward them. If it is fair to call this orneriness "conservative," then it helps clarify traditional conservatism's sharp divergence from liberalism and from this essay.

Beyond this, there are some essential functions that only government is likely to be prepared to perform (collecting garbage) and services it may be best placed to manage, if not necessarily perform itself (public transport, road systems, and utilities). And finally, there may be very rare instances in which the case is overwhelming for government to manage or provide services that are not essential but are highly desirable and would be delivered much less well and much less in our interest by other means, notably medicare; or directly to fund jobs, as Keynes would have us do during recessions (and *only* during recessions, I might add); or even to undertake major economic projects where national survival or pre-eminent national interests are at stake. With these, however, we are very much at the outer limit of the powers that ought to be left with governments.

Limiting government is crucial. Shearing from it the mess of programmes by which governments have tried to skew the market, manage the economy, control social forces and compete actively in the market is very important in returning government to sanity and in saving resources that are being wasted. Dropping superfluous, expensive, wasteful and misguided functions is the first consequence we would expect to flow from better management in government, management that is much more clear-sighted and even ruthless about what it is possible and affordable to do and what not. There is a central need to

- make management in government strategic and priority-driven;
- alter internal budgetary systems to encourage saving and effective use of funds rather than, as now, their waste;
- identify the business processes of government, organize the bureaucracy

around them, and make them a great deal more efficient, less hierarchical and more client-oriented;
- make the outputs of these processes more measurable so that we can tell success from failure in government businesses;
- aggressively seek ways to put power and responsibility back into individual hands, as in the school system and retirement income, to take two examples; and
- radically reform the administrative, personnel, and control edifice in government, so that it ceases to be a tool for obtaining and holding internal power and actually promotes efficiency and client-service.

Government will still have many important things to do and it must do them a great deal better if it is to serve the interests of its public in more palpable ways than it does now.

Governments that are constructed on these lines are not nearly so likely to end up with massive public indebtedness. Since we are in a mess, however, we have no alternative over the short term but to dig ourselves out of it. You and I must consistently urge responsible management on governments, and vote them out of office whenever they fail to heed us, until things have been set right. We must constantly oppose tax increases as a means of getting government off the hook and challenge the arrogance of our leaders whenever they think they can get away with another round. We are overtaxed and overgoverned as it is. We must insist on the primacy of our interests and deny that governments exist to serve anything more important than themselves. On the other hand, cleaning up the mess is our first task. Those who talk about tax reductions before this is achieved are irresponsible. Those reductions must come some day soon, as part of the type of overhaul of government this essay recommends, but in the meantime, we all have to pay for over a generation of imprudence.

This raises one final thought. We all share the responsibility for the mess we are in and, as a consequence, for the need to clean it up. We blame our governments, and while they have not done very well by us, they got us into trouble partly because we willingly acquiesced in their grand plans and demanded more from them than they were capable of giving or than was good for us. Let us never forget that we individuals are the most important constituents of our political community and that we have the greatest responsibility to set it right. If we abdicate that responsibility to governments, we can hardly complain when they do not take it very seriously. It was Mill who wrote, "The worth of a State, in the long run, is the worth of the individuals composing it."[1]

It is essential that we get on with the business of reform quickly, for every day lost is a tragedy for the future of our country and for our children, who shall go on for their lifetimes paying the price of our profligacy.

NOTES

Chapter 1: Where Will It All End?

1. These sources appear in the Selected Bibliography. I will not refer to specific volumes or page numbers.
2. These are not defined very precisely and I use them mostly for purposes of comparison. I have endeavoured to ensure that different approaches to compilation of the lists of departments and agencies in Almanacs prepared forty years apart from each other have been taken into account. Some of the more independent Crown corporations, such as CNR, appeared in neither volume.
3. A difficulty in comparing the numbers is that there was a very sizeable class of "temporary" employees in 1950, people who worked most, but not all, of the mandatory hours in a week. I have converted these to what are now called "Full-Time Equivalents" (FTEs) by dividing their number by the average salary for permanent employees.
4. The number of civilians is in fact:
   Permanent 45,259
   Temporary 81,937
   Since the average annual wage of permanent workers was $2,648, I have converted the temporaries to the equivalent of $61,867 full-time.
5. Figures may be read in various ways. I recently saw an article asserting that federal government employment actually declined by 4 per cent between 1974 and 1993. Once all the scrutiny is done to figure out what really occurred – and I rather suspect that more decline has been loaded into the last few years than into the first fifteen – it is probably true enough that restraint has had its effects at the Federal level. The overall cost of personnel, on the other hand, must have increased voluminously until the last few years of wage freeze.
6. Besides the Canada Yearbooks, a useful summary of statistical information that contains, among other things, GDP/GNP conversions, is F.H. Leacy, ed., *Historical Statistics of Canada* (2nd ed.), Statistics Canada, Ottawa, 1983.
7. Municipal expenditures are not given for 1950 in the earlier yearbooks and are estimated on the basis of revenues.
8. Quoted in *The Globe and Mail*, 27 June 1994.
9. An article by April Lindgren in the *Ottawa Citizen*, 10 February 1995, pp. 1-2, quoting OECD figures, does not put the figure quite so high: 36.1 per cent of GDP, about average for OECD countries, although Canada has increased faster than all the others except Italy during the last decade. Other sources still use the higher figure. My point, in any case, is not that Canada is worse than all or most of the others; it is that taxation's share of GDP is colossal and out of control in Canada, and for that matter, in almost all of the democratic world.
10. "Hot Dog Tax Hazards," *Ottawa Business Magazine* (Rick Sutcliffe, ed.), Ottawa, Winter 1995, p. 10.
11. A report early in 1994 said it had reached 97 per cent. By September, reports were already saying it equals GDP. A recent controversy over OECD statistics put the figure in the mid-80s; I take this to be net national debt, that is gross national debt minus cash and other assets in the government's hands.
12. The Canada Yearbook number. *Historical Statistics of Canada* puts it at $18.491 billion.
13. In fact, savings were found within government programmes to fuel the infrastructure projects, but these savings could have been used to reduce debt.

Chapter 2: Exposing Leviathan

1. *Leviathan*, Bobbs-Merrill, Indianapolis, New York, 1958, pp. 105-106.
2. A full account of this appears in *Creating a Government that Works Better & Costs Less: Report of the National Performance Review*, USA: Washington, 1993.
3. Budgeting is done on the basis of longer-term, traditionally five-year (now usually three-year), planning cycles and projects may be spread over several years. However, money may only be allocated annually in most instances. Uncertainty, short-term perspectives and loss of investment in abandoned projects often prevail.
4. Broadly, zero-based budgeting is the rejustification from the ground up of all programmes each year; single operating budgets unite salary, operating and capital budgets, leaving to the manager the decision as to how best to divide his loot.
5. The 1995 budget, in fact, makes some improvements. It imposes real reduction targets on departmental budgets, not fantasy reductions based on growth scenarios. Thus, the message is clear that there are no new or additional funds for which departments can compete. However, there remains no incentive for managers to reduce.

Chapter 3: Organization Men

1. Robert P. Reid Jr., George Washington University, quoted from an address. "There's More to Quality Than Quality Management," at the Seventh Annual National Conference on Federal Quality, September, 1994.
2. Leviathan, practically everywhere, but see, for example, p. 106: " ... In the nature of man we find three principal causes of quarrel, first, competition; secondly, diffidence; thirdly, glory."

Chapter 4: The Role of Government

1. Especially pp. 160–67.
2. An example is official travel, in which, at the time of writing, compliance with multitudes of rules continues to elbow out less intrusive, cheaper approaches (fixed per diem and travel allowances, elimination of accounting, etc.).

Chapter 5: Out of Business

1. There are a number of standard, if rather complicated, descriptions of the terms and conditions of the CPP. I have used a publication of the Office of the Superintendent of Financial Institutions, *Canada Pension Plan: Fifteenth Actuarial Report as at 31 December 1993, Ottawa, 1995.*
2. I refer in particular to "The burden of our pensions" (15 August 1994, p. A8). The other articles in the *Globe's* series ran as follows: "Canada's other national debt: the tension in pensions" 13–17 August 1995; "Let's give more to the old and poor and less to the old and rich" (13 August 1994, p. D1); "How the CPP can be fixed" (16 August 1994, p. A6); "Let's create a nation that saves" (17 August 1994, p. A5).
3. A middle income earner may average about $3,000 a year in payments into the Public Service Superannuation Plan, for example. These are matched by her employer. The total value of her contributions might reach $100,000 after thirty years service but she would be eligible for an annual pension equal to 60 per cent of the average salary of her best six years, some $40,000. if she earned between $60,000 – $70,000.
4. There is a minute Death Benefit, a maximum of $3,490 in 1995.
5. I mean for minimum contributions designed to ensure income in retirement comparable to the CPP, not for RRSPs as a whole.

Chapter 6: Education

1. 2 October 1994, p. A9.
2. Eric Beauchesne, "Canada near top of class on spending for education," Ottawa Citizen, 12 April 1995.
3. In "Public schools can accommodate more options for students."
4. The other two are "Choices would increase accountability" by Elaine Hopkins and "'Associate schools' offer a compromise" by McGill Principal Bernard Shapiro.
5. I do not want to be unfair. Governments are failing to enforce decent standards in part because their constituents are not insistent enough on having them. Ex premier Rae was recently excoriated in the press for criticizing poor performance by students in province-wide tests because he was challenging a "delicate compromise" in the community over whether there should have been such tests at all!
6. Probably a new system would allow us an opportunity to do in the property tax system, at least for funding school boards.
7. Op. cit., pp. 194ff.

Chapter 7: Efficiency in the Public Service

1. A summary of the development of the business process concept may be found in Ole Ingstrup, *Reengineering in the Public Service: Promise or Peril?* Explorations no. 6, Canadian Centre for Management Development, Ottawa, 1995. Ingstrup is the principal of CCMD.
2. *Reengineering the Corporation*, Harper Business, New York, 1993.
3. Not everyone agrees with the picture of hierarchical management I have offered. See, for example, Elliott Jacques, "In Praise of Hierarchy," Harvard Business Review, January - February 1990, pp. 127–33. Jacques' argument is rather theoretical, it seems to me, and he underestimates the success of new, more fluid organizational forms, though he is right to point out their embryonic nature. Interestingly, his account of problems in hierarchical organization are closely parallel to some of those discussed in Chapter Two.
4. I am referring to Chaper Two.
5. I do not underestimate the extent of opposition to this notion from either the personnel bureaucracies or the unions.
6. Speech to the APEX Symposium, Ottawa, 16 May 1994.

Chapter 8: Old Liberalism

1. John Stuart Mill, long ago, foresaw this in strikingly modern terms in the last chapter of *On Liberty*, in *Utilitarianism, Liberty* and *Representative Government* (ed. A.D. Lindsay), London, 1910, pp. 165ff.
2. I have used an old textbook, *The Second Treatise of Government*, Bobbs-Merrill, Indianapolis and New York, 1952.
3. Ibid, p. 72.
4. p. 10.
5. p. 79, 80.
6. This is not to deny great differences between them. As Mill points out, Locke posited the social contract so as to deduce political rights and obligations from it. Mill defines rights in more immediately personal and moral terms.
7. On Liberty, p. 115.
8. p. 132.
9. pp. 72-73.
10. In a passage from which one of the following quotations is taken appears the characterization of a constitution "dependent on the voluntary surrender by the different members of the community of their individual freedom of action."
11. pp. 118-19.
12. pp. 197-98.
13. *On Liberty*, p. 195.
14. pp. 150-51.
15. Pierre Elliot Trudeau, of course.
16. Canadian historian Michael Bliss has recently put this thesis into a readable form in his article, "Canada's Swell War," *Saturday Night*, 110, no. 4, Toronto, May 1995: 38-41, 64.
17. Subtitled: *The Defeat of Canadian Nationalism*, McClelland and Stewart, Toronto, 1965.
18. Straussianism will be an uncommon "ism" to many readers. I refer to the philosopher Leo Strauss, a charismatic teacher and a Platonist, whose followers include Grant.
19. Op cit., p. 48, for example.
20. I do not accept the fairness of this criticism. Locke

was aware of the criticism that no state of nature had ever existed and dealt with it with considerable sophistication, suggesting that he did not himself believe in the state of nature literally but saw it as something that some real-life societies might approximate. See pp. 56ff.

21. See for example the early sections of Karl Marx and Friedrich Engels, *The German Ideology*, International Publishers, New York, 1947, pp. 6ff.
22. Michael Reed, *The Georgian Triumph 1700-1830*, Granada, London, 1984, pp. 30-31.
23. *On Liberty*, p. 151.
24. Clarendon Press, Oxford, 1958.
25. Subtitled *A Political Memoir*, Weidenfeld & Nicolson, London, 1980.

Chapter 9: New Liberalism: Freedom of the Individual

1. I sidestep a very complex matter. In some societies, in particular primitive societies, "freedom" may be a concept with no meaning. Other "collectivist" societies, like the Confucian ones, may put a lower priority on freedom than on other "goods," like solidarity. Arbitrary oppression may be more acceptable to people in these societies than in ours. However, would anyone wish to argue on this basis that it is right?
2. Hayek, for example.
3. Op. cit., p. 131.
4. The intellectual left does not agree. It considers that government interventions of various kinds have been decisive in bringing prosperity to the working class, suggesting that workers were barely better off in 1900 than they were in 1800, or at any rate had not increased their share of the national income. See Peter Laslett, for example, in *The World We Have Lost*, London, 1968, p. 220 in particular. However, even if this is wrong and Pareto's Law true, we should not ignore the complex set of factors that led to improved conditions for the working classes nor the value of social security programmes in mitigating their hardships.
5. **Ø See above, p. 105**
6. University of Chicago Press, Chicago, 1994 (Fiftieth Anniversary Edition: the original was published in England in 1944).
7. Interestingly, John Stuart Mill uses an argument rather like this in defence of enfranchising the working class and other propertyless persons. Op. cit., p. 209, in *Representative Government*.
8. A figure of $120 million annually has been estimated for Ontario.

Chapter 10: New Liberalism: Limiting Government

1. Macmillan: Toronto, 1968.
2. For example, Donald J. Savoie in "Globalization and Governance," Research Paper no. 12, Canadian Centre for Management Development, Ottawa, 1993.
3. Such as John Rawls' use of contract theory in *A Theory of Justice*, Belknaps, Cambridge (Mass.), 1971.
4. Thirty years ago, political science came close to endorsing such an ideology, for example, Seymour Martin Lipset in *Political Man*. (I oversimplify, of course, and do little justice to one of the great political scientists of this century, whose analysis, indeed, has more truth in it than we might like to admit.) It saw the absence of activism and political ignorance in a large segment of society as an actual benefit, a guarantee of stability. Heaven help us, it was said, if everyone shared the activism of the handful of people who make politics a central part of their lives. Leave politics to the elites, who generate conflict and instability enough. The ignorant, the lower orders of society, bring authoritarian assumptions and oversimplifications to politics. They turn into mobs.
5. We tend to think of these as being in the economic sphere, and to be sure, the creation of businesses and enterprises is a prime example. However, social innovation can include any sphere, new religious movements, for example. If one thinks of their longevity, institutions like monasticism and churches must be counted as among the most "successful" of any we know about, outliving all political and economic institutions.

Chapter 11: Jumping to Conclusions

1. Op. cit., p.170 (in the conclusion of *On Liberty*).

SELECTED BIBLIOGRAPHY

Beauchesne, Eric. "Canada near top of class on spending for education." *The Ottawa Citizen*, April 12, 1995: p. A4.

Berlin, Isaiah. *Two Concepts of Liberty*. Clarendon Press: Oxford, 1958.

Bliss, Michael. "Canada's Swell War." *Saturday Night* (Kenneth Whyte, ed.), 110, no. 4 (May 1995): 38-41, 64.

Bourgon, Jocelyne. Speech to the APEX Symposium. Ottawa, May 16, 1994.

Canada. *Canada Pension Plan: Fifteenth Actuarial Report as at 31 December 1995*. Office of the Superintendent of Financial Institutions Canada: Ottawa, 1995.

Canada. *Canada Yearbook 1951*. Ottawa, 1951.

Canada. *Canada Yearbook 1952–53*. Ottawa, 1953.

Canada. *Canada Yearbook 1993*. Ottawa, 1993.

Canada. *Historical Statistics of Canada* (2nd edition) (F.H. Leacy, ed.). Statistics Canada: Ottawa, 1983.

Canadian Almanac and Directory 1950 (Marsh Jeanneret, ed.). Copp Clark: Toronto, 1950.

Canadian Almanac and Directory 1990 (Susan Bracken, ed.). Copp Clark Pitman: Toronto 1990.

Coyne, Andrew. "The burden of our pensions." *The Globe and Mail* [Toronto], August 15, 1994: p. A8.

Dobell, Jane. "Public schools can accommodate more options for students." *The Ottawa Citizen*, October 2, 1994: p. A9.

Douglas, Roger. *Unfinished Business*. Random House New Zealand: Auckland, 1993.

Drucker, Peter. *Post-Capitalist Society*. Harper Business: New York, 1995.

Gore, Vice President Al. *Creating a Government that Works Better and Costs Less: Report of the National Performance Review*. Washington, 1993.

Grant, George. *Lament for a Nation: The Defeat of Canadian Nationalism*. McClelland and Stewart: Toronto, 1965.

Hammer, Michael, and Champy James. *Reengineering the Corporation*. Harper Business: New York, 1993.

Hayek, F.A. *The Road to Serfdom.* University of Chicago Press: Chicago, 1994 (Fiftieth Anniversary edition).

Hobbes, Thomas. *Leviathan.* Bobbs-Merrill: Indianapolis, New York, 1958.

Hopkins, Elaine. "Choices would increase accountability." *The Ottawa Citizen,* October 2, 1994: p. A9.

Ingstrup, Ole. "Reengineering in the Public Service: Promise or Peril?" *Explorations No. 6.* Canadian Centre for Management Development: Ottawa, 1995.

Jacques, Elliott. "In Praise of Hierarchy." *Harvard Business Review,* 68, (January – February 1990): 127–33.

Lindgren, April. "Grass-Roots Revolt Based on High-Tax Myth." *The Ottawa Citizen,* February 10, 1995: pp. 1–2.

Locke, John. *The Second Treatise of Government.* Bobbs-Merrill: Indianapolis and New York, 1952.

Massé, Marcel. "The Renewal of Government: An Evolving Strategy." Speech to the Apex Symposium. Ottawa, May 10, 1994.

Mill, John Stuart. *Utilitarianism, Liberty and Representative Government* (A.D. Lindsay, ed.). J.M. Dent, London and E.P Dutton: New York, 1910.

Peters, Tom. *Liberation Management.* Fawcett Columbine: New York, 1992.

Podhoretz, Norman. *Breaking Ranks: A Political Memoir.* Weidenfeld & Nicolson: London, 1979.

Reed, Michael. *The Georgian Triumph 1700–1830.* Granada: London, 1983.

Reid, Robert P., Jr. "There's More to Quality Than Quality Management." Address to the Seventh Annual National Conference on Federal Quality, September 1994.

Savoie, Donald J. "Globalization and Governance." *Research Paper No. 12.* Canadian Centre for Management Development: Ottawa, 1993.

Shapiro, Frank. "'Associate schools' offer a compromise." *The Ottawa Citizen,* October 2, 1994: p. A9.

Sutcliffe, Rick, ed. "Hot Dog Tax Hazards." *Ottawa Business Magazine.* Pegasus, Winter, 1995: p. 10.

Trudeau, Pierre Elliott. *Federalism and the French-Canadians* (John Saywell, ed.). Macmillan: Toronto, 1968.

Index